Inside Fly Tying

Inside Fly Tying

100 TIPS FOR SOLVING
THE TRICKIEST
FLY-TYING PROBLEMS

Dick Talleur

STACKPOLE
BOOKS

Published by
STACKPOLE BOOKS
5067 Ritter Road
Mechanicsburg, PA 17055
www.stackpolebooks.com

Printed in China

First edition

10 9 8 7 6 5 4 3 2 1

Cover photographs by the author
Cover design by Tracy Patterson

Library of Congress Cataloging-in-Publication Data

Talleur, Richard W.
    Inside fly tying : 100 tips for solving the trickiest fly-tying problems / Dick Talleur.—1st ed.
        p. cm.
    Includes index.
    ISBN 0-8117-3138-3 (alk. paper)
    1. Fly tying. I. Title.
SH451 .T2875 2004
688.7'9124—dc22
                                    2003025413

Contents

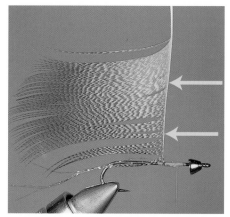

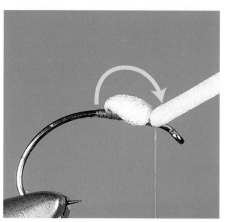

Preface

As many of you know, I've written a number of books on fly tying, and many articles about that subject. Why another one, and what makes this book different? The answer is threefold:

1. To demonstrate the benefits of certain newer materials.
2. To take advantage of new graphics technology, in order to go into detail on specific techniques that make fly tying easier and produce better results.
3. To acquaint readers with some new patterns and designs that I have either originated or contributed to the evolution of.

This is a book I've wanted to write for a long time. Thanks to contemporary methods in computer graphics and photo reproduction, I am now able to portray fly-tying details as never before. Don't let words like "detail" and "precision" scare you; employing such techniques makes tying easier, not harder. My experience in teaching fly tying for well over a quarter of a century has proven this many times over.

The information given herein will benefit both beginning tiers and more experienced ones, including even advanced tiers. I can't present, in a single volume, everything that's newer and better. Fly tying has become far too vast for that, and no one tier can be the authority on everything. What I want to show here is what I believe will help the largest majority of tiers with the problems they encounter most frequently. Simply stated, this is the stuff that I think is the most important.

Not all of the flies you'll see here are new, nor are all of the techniques; in fact, a number of them appear in my previous books (winging a dry fly, for example). I repeat them here because:

1. I want to use new graphics to show these techniques in high detail and clarity.
2. I want to include certain fundamentals for the elucidation of new tiers, of which there are many.
3. I want to show how certain components, such as the Wulff-style wing and the wood duck wing, integrate with other components of the fly.
4. Based on my experiences in the many tying classes I teach, I see that winging dry flies gives people bigger problems than almost anything else.

All of the patterns presented herein are flies I have fished and experienced success with. Also, they are good "teaching" flies—that is, they enable me to clearly convey the details, the little nuances that make tying easier and flies come out better. The fish may not care—but we do, right? I don't know of a single tier who doesn't take pride in his or her flies, and I know from personal experience that liking the fly you tie to your leader results in more confident and effective fishing.

This is a book of not only hows but whys. My teaching experience has convinced me that people do better when they understand the reasoning behind specific instructions. Sometimes—especially with those new to tying—things that cause difficulties are not readily apparent, and the tier struggles on, thinking it's a shortcoming on his or her part. But that's not it! Here's an example: Some years ago, I convinced a student, already a pretty good tier, that he should buy some high-grade dry-fly capes that were on display in the store where I was teaching a weekend class. A week or so later, he called me on the phone and complained that the feathers weren't wrapping as neatly and easily as I had promised him they would. After some back-and-forth, I gave him one instruction: Be sure to strip the feathers all the way back to the "sweet spot," where the quill was fine and flexible and the barbs were prime.

A half hour later, he called back and said the problem was solved and the feathers were behaving wonderfully. He had simply been so anxious to use every single bit of the feathers he had paid good money for that he wasn't discarding the portion lower down on the quill. This is a very common and serious mistake. Think about it; if you try to use too much of the feather, the thicker quill with poorer-quality barbs gets wrapped first and will virtually fill up the space allocated for hackle, so there's no room left for the high-quality stuff farther out into the feather!

So with each tying sequence, I'll state what potential problems or challenges are likely to be encountered, and give my recommendations for solving them. I hope this makes your tying a successful and rewarding experience.

To thank everyone who has contributed to my development as a fly tier would require a book in and of itself. However, I want to acknowledge certain individuals who have been of significance in recent years and have become great friends and fishing companions of mine. I'll probably forget some deserving souls; please forgive me.

Nick Wilder, proprietor of Hunter's Angling Supplies, for providing me with an excellent teaching venue, where I was able not only to teach, but to learn from teaching.

Dick Soares of the Manchester, New Hampshire, area for constructive criticism, rekindling my enthusiasm, and being a great boat partner and friend.

Sim Savage of Portland, Maine, for sharing patterns and tying tips and for wonderful angling companionship and friendship.

Marla Blair, lady guide from Ludlow, Massachusetts, for showing me the Jailbird pattern and how to fish it on the challenging rivers she guides on, and for being such a fun companion.

Dr. Tom Whiting of Delta, Colorado, master of advance chicken culture, for supporting my sometimes-experimental efforts and enabling me to enjoy the advantages of tying with the best feather materials in the history of fly tying.

Wally Baker, Bill Chase, and everyone at Anglers' Sport Group in Elba, New York, for supporting my teaching and writing efforts by helping with those wonderful Daiichi hooks.

Paul Betters, the founding proprietor of Anglers' Sport Group, who recruited me back in 1991 into what turned out to be an enduring symbiotic relationship.

Jean-Guy Cote, proprietor of the Uni Corporation of St. Melanie, Quebec, for supplying excellent products: Uni-Thread, Uni-Stretch, Uni-Yarn, and other fine stuff.

Barry Nation, manager of Rivers Camera, Rochester, New Hampshire, for all of his help with photography and photographic equipment.

Lee and Art Stoliar, the Fly Tyer's Carryall people, who produce the Folstaff and other fine items for the angler, for many years of support and friendship.

Bill Black and the Spirit River Company for their generosity in providing me with their exceptionally well-thought-out fly-tying materials and implements.

May the God of Your Persuasion bless you all.

Dick Talleur
Manchester, New Hampshire
Summer 2003

Talleur's Tying Tips

1

Before we get into the particulars of specific tying techniques, here are some general instructions that I believe will serve you well.

1. Think like a pool player. In billiards, the shot at hand sets up those to come. Likewise, in fly tying, the operation at hand affects subsequent ones. For example, in the following chapters, you'll see how the shaping and integration of the wing and tail butts on dry flies set up a neat, even foundation for the body.

2. Be circumspect when purchasing critical materials. Bargain hunting is fine, provided you know one when you see one. Prime dry-fly hackle, such as the Whiting Farms products, may seem pricey, but their exceptionally high yield makes them a very good buy.

3. Choose your working threads with discretion. The wide variety of threads available today enables you to optimize your selection on a task-oriented basis. And don't hesitate to change threads during the course of tying a particular fly. For example, in the stonefly nymph chapter, you start with Uni-Stretch, which serves as both the body material and working thread. Then, midway through the fly, you switch to regular thread, in this case, 8/0 Uni-Thread. This reduces bulk.

4. Develop sound thread management. In the forthcoming chapters, you'll see references to such thread management techniques as the pinch, the soft wrap, the gathering wrap, and the distribution wrap. All of these are task-related; often gentle "gathering" wraps or soft loops work much better than making tight wraps, using all the tension the thread will bear.

5. Learn to analyze materials from the standpoint of how they will behave in actual use. Lots of stuff looks great in the package and on the wall but doesn't work on the fly. Dubbings are a prime example. Often it's hard to tell just by looking at the package what sort of texture they have or how long the strands are. A great deal can be learned at the numerous shows where top tiers exhibit their skills. Watch them, and don't be afraid to ask questions; usually you'll get a most helpful response.

6. When using dubbing, choose the type that's right for the job. Unless you're tying a unique, materials-specific dressing—Hare's Ear is a good example—it doesn't matter whether your dubbing is natural or synthetic. What does matter is its texture and working characteristics.

7. Regardless of type, all dubbings work best when applied gradually, in small wisps, so that maximum thread contact is obtained. This is true in both single-thread and dubbing-loop operations.

8. Pay strict attention to proportions. If the components on a particular fly are not sized properly, the design of the fly and its size are compromised, and it may not float or balance as desired. For example, a conventional dry fly should rest on the tips of the tail and hackle, with the hook barely touching or just clearing a flat surface. Also important: The wings must not be too high or too heavily dressed, and the tail should be spread to create a "snowshoe" effect, and also should not contain more material than needed.

9. Think about what sort of knot you'll be using when fishing a fly. This will affect your choice of hook and how much space you leave at the eye.

10. When working near the eye of the hook, it's helpful to do the final thread operations opposite from the way the hook eye is bent. On a down-eye hook, tie off on top, and on an up-eye hook, vice versa.

11. Fly tying can be a wonderful art form, and I appreciate that as much as anyone. However, remember that the fish don't go to shows and museums, and they are not art critics. If you're tying flies for the water, tie them for the fish, rather than for the wall. It's a question of function and feasibility. To illustrate the point: Tying time for a full-dress Green Highlander is around two hours—for me, at least. For the reduced hair-wing version, it's twelve to fifteen minutes.

12. Buy good tools. If you're a beginner, don't spend a lot of money until you have a thorough understanding of the requisite tools, their functions, and their points of quality. Ask for help from a knowledgeable friend, and don't take ads or sales pitches at face value. Don't assume that costlier is better, or that more complex is more functional. There are some very acceptable tools, even vises, available at reasonable cost. However, also be aware that the cheapest is often the worst. Keep your mind open to innovation, but be skeptical of gimmicks. Scissors and hackle pliers are prime examples.

13. Seek help from experienced tiers—but be sure they are qualified to give advice. And remember, there are very few absolutes in fly tying. Once the basics are mastered, the field is open for you to develop your own methods and techniques. But be self-critical; if something isn't working to your satisfaction, explore alternatives.

Hackle Selection

We'll begin with a brief orientation in the understanding and selection of feathers for hackling dry flies. Good technique will partially compensate for poor-quality hackle, but why fight it? Buy the right stuff, and delight in the results.

Size (barb length) and quality may be judged by flexing feathers into a simulation of the wrapped position they will assume on the hook. It's okay to do this in a fly shop, provided it is done with care, so that there is no damage whatsoever to the pelt. Saddle hackles can be deceptive, in that the barbs resist protruding straight out from the quill when flexed. The higher the quality, the more this is the case. The illusion that results is that the barbs appear shorter than they will come out in actual use, when wrapped around a hook.

GENERAL ATTRIBUTES OF QUALITY HACKLE

1. Very fine, flexible quills.
2. Stiff, strong barbs, relatively web-free.
3. High barb count—that is, a dense deployment of barbs on the quill.
4. Consistency of barb length, which is what determines size.
5. Beautiful coloration or sheen.
6. Equal barb length on both sides of the quill.

A comment about that last item. If the barbs on a feather are only slightly unequal in length on either side of the quill, that's okay. If there is more than a slight disparity, I'd suggest that you not use such feathers for tying standard hackles. However, they can be used for parachute hackles.

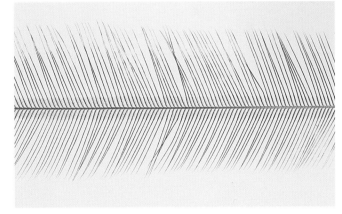

Watch out for feathers having unequal barb length on either side of the quill. A little is allowable. More than that, as seen here, is okay for parachutes.

Sizing hackles can be tricky. At first glance, this feather appeared to be a size 14, but it turned out to be a solid size 12.

ATTRIBUTES OF NECKS/CAPES

1. Wide range of sizes.
2. Long "sweet spots," meaning quality throughout a large portion of the feather.
3. Presence of tailing material around the edges.
4. Bonus: streamer, wet fly hackle at the rear.

These are both very good-quality feathers. The grizzly on the left has a higher barb count, and the barbs are a little stronger.

Typical range of sizes on a good-quality cape: size 22 up to size 10.

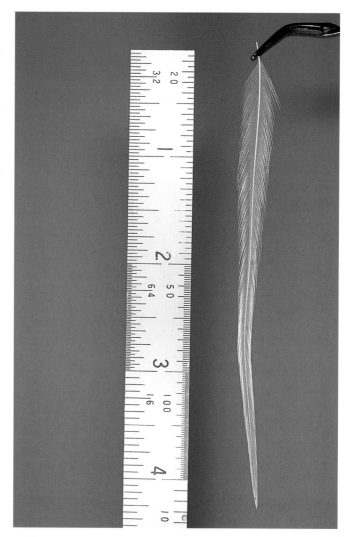

A fine-quality cape feather, before the "sweet spot" is isolated.

ATTRIBUTES OF SADDLES

1. Quality extends well down the feather, almost to the butt end.
2. Size range (limited on saddles).
3. Straight barbs (not cupped).
4. Barbs same length on either side of the quill.
5. Consistency of barb length throughout the length of the feather.
6. Bonus: wet fly and Woolly Bugger hackle in the center of the pelt.

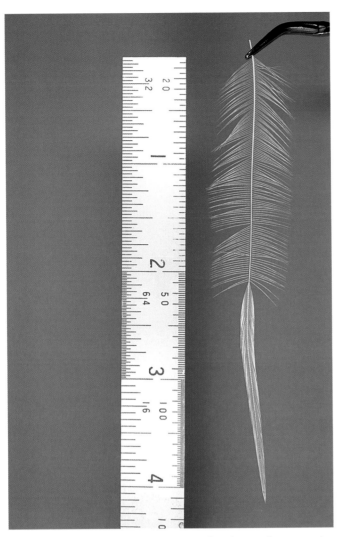

The same feather. The barbs that are flared must be stripped off. What's left is prime hackle: the sweet spot.

A beautiful cree rooster cape from Whiting Farms. Very scarce.

NOTES AND OBSERVATIONS

1. When selecting capes and/or saddles, be sure to judge size in the *quality portion* of the feather—that which will actually form the hackle. Take your time, and look at lots of feathers in different portions of the pelt.
2. When selecting pelts that are to be used together, such as a brown and a grizzly for the Adams, it's recommended that this be done concurrently, so that uniformity and compatibility can be assured.
3. There are often noticeable differences in quality between grizzly saddles and other colors, especially with Whiting Farms products, with their ongoing development of the Hoffman line of barred rocks. This is due to very selective breeding, and also because grizzly birds naturally grow better saddle hackles than other strains. It's important to be aware of this factor, especially if you are going to be matching up feathers from a grizzly saddle with those from brown and other colored saddles.
4. It is okay to mix saddle and cape feathers on a fly if the size and characteristics are generally compatible.
5. When sizing a feather for hackling a particular fly, keep in mind that you must add in whatever buildup of materials has accrued where the hackle will be wrapped, as this in effect increases the size of the hackle. On larger flies where bulky materials have been used, this can be significant.

The chapters to follow will demonstrate how to make dry-fly hackles using both cape and saddle feathers.

A Wulff-Style Dry Fly

By not crowding the hook eye, a proper Turle-type knot can easily be formed, where the loop passes around the neck of the fly, and the knot itself stays at the throat, behind the eye.

S everal of fly tying's most valuable techniques and disciplines are epitomized in tying the dry fly, so let's make that our first tying exercise. We'll begin with a hair-winged pattern, as it uses the same sorts of materials and methods as the Wulff family—and that includes some of the most productive, time-tested patterns in fly fishing.

IN THIS CHAPTER YOU'LL LEARN

1. Securing and configuring the hair, or Wulff-style, wing.
2. Shaping the underbody.
3. Dry-fly dubbing.
4. Setting the stage for the hackle.
5. The hackle tie-in.
6. Wrapping the Wulff hackle with a single feather.
7. The "clean" tie-off and finish knot.

A word about that last note: So far as I can deduce, the main reason that so many hooks have turned-down eyes is to accommodate the ever-popular Improved Turle Knot. When this knot is properly tied, the loop passes over the "neck" of the fly, and the knot itself stays at the "throat," in back of the eye. If you crowd the head area when tying off, that makes it almost impossible to tighten the knot without everything slipping over the front.

This Turle knot is formed improperly; the loop has slipped over the head of the fly, and the entire knot ends up in front. This weakens the knot.

EXPLANATIONS

Q. Why apply the dubbing with the thread advanced a few turns ahead of the starting point?

A. Because it's hard to spin on the material right up to the hook shank; the hook point and front end of the vise get in the way. This technique allows for wrapping back a few turns to the bend, at which point the dubbing will be in position to start wrapping the body.

Q. What's the proper length of the wrapped hackle?

A. About one and a half times the hook gape. This balances the fly, so that it will float on the tips of the hackle and tail.

Q. Why leave a tiny bit of the bare quill exposed at the hackle tie-in point?

A. Because this allows the quill to rotate to 90 degrees, so that the beginning wrap of hackle stands straight out, and not laid back at an angle.

Q. Why wrap the hackle feather bright-side-forward?

A. So that the barbs stand straight, rather than lean forward. Keep in mind that the feather is shaped to fit the body of a chicken.

Q. Why the back-and-forth wrapping method?

A. To create a denser hackle, which is desirable on Wulff-type flies.

Q. Why tie off the hackle on top of the hook?

A. Because it's much easier to keep the hook eye clear by making the whip-finish knot away from the eye area.

UP-CHUCK

I have named this fly the Up-Chuck, because it's a good floater and, therefore, "up" on the surface, and the wings and tail are made of woodchuck hair. This is one of my patterns—I think. One never knows what all those other creative tiers out there may have conjured up.

Hook:	Dry fly; here, a Daiichi model 1180.
Thread:	Fire orange 8/0 Uni-Thread or comparable.
Wings and tail:	Woodchuck guard hairs.
Body:	Rusty tan dubbing.
Hackle:	Cree, or other multicolored barred hackle.

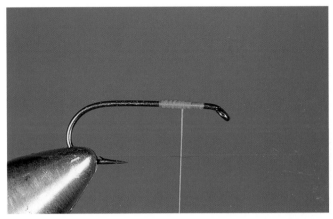

1. Wrap a substantial thread base or foundation: three or four layers. Note that the thread ends up in the center of the foundation, about 30 percent of the shank length to the rear of the hook eye. This allows for wrapping the hackle in front of the wings and having room to tie off.

2. Cut off a small bunch of hair from a woodchuck pelt, and remove the underfur so that only the guard hairs remain. A fine-tooth comb is helpful for this.

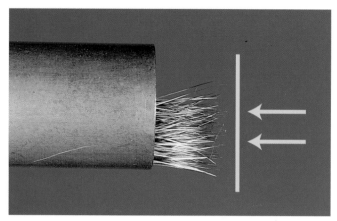

3. Even up the tip ends with a hair-evening tool, commonly called a stacker. Note that the hair is pointing in the direction in which it will be tied on to form the wings, so you don't have to turn it around with your fingers and risk messing it up.

6. Be sure the hair bunch is securely tied on. Then, using your thumb, crimp the hair bunch into an upright position. This gives the hair some "memory" and prepares it for the next step.

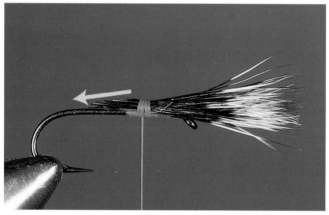

4. The wings should be the same length as the hook shank, meaning that portion from the eye to the beginning of the bend. Tie in the hair on top of the hook. The arrow indicates how the hair butts are taper-cut.

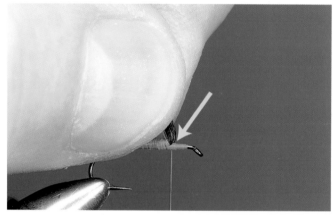

7. Stand the hair up straight by building a "dam" of thread. It's essential to wrap plenty of thread tight to the front of the hair, but in the process, make smoothing wraps back and forth toward the eye.

5. Cover the taper-cut wing butts neatly with thread. This is step 1 in creating a smooth underbody.

8. View the hair bunch from the top, and with a pointed instrument of some sort, divide the hair into two equal bunches. Then separate them by making one or two **X** wraps, crossing front-to-back-to-front between the wings-to-be.

9. Use at least two figure-eight wraps to permanently configure and position the wings. First, the far wing: Start with the thread in front of the wings, cross front-to-back between the wings, firmly grasp the hair by the tip, then wrap the thread around just the *base of the hair* (not the hook) 360 degrees, coming back between the wings, *maintaining firm thread tension throughout*. Don't let go of the bobbin until the thread is hanging straight down behind the near wing on the near side of the hook.

10. Now for the near wing: Wrap around the *base of the hair* (not the hook) 360 degrees, coming forward between the wings, *maintaining firm thread tension throughout*. Don't let go of the bobbin until the thread is hanging straight down in front of the far wing on the far side of the hook.

11. A front view of the wings, showing the spread.

12. Cut off a small bunch of hair for the tail, and stack the tips as before. Point the stacker such that the tips of the hair bunch will be pointing rearward. The tail should be just a bit longer than the hook shank, so use that as a guide. Slope-cut the butts so they dovetail with the wing butts.

13. The completed tail should be just a bit longer than the hook shank.

14. Advance the thread a few turns forward, as it is hard to spin dubbing right up against the hook shank. Spin on a thin layer of the body material. The toothpick in the photo is there for perspective, to show the thickness of the dubbing.

15. Take a few thread wraps rearward so that the dubbing starts at the bend, where the tail departs from the hook.

16. Wrap the body.

17. Leave space behind the wing for the hackle.

18. Here, a single saddle feather will be used to hackle the fly; thus, this is a departure from the traditional back-to-front hackling technique. Choose a feather of the proper size by flexing it into a simulation of the wrapped position so the barbs are flared. Strip the excess barbs from the base of the hackle feather to remove any soft, webby material. Then tie in the feather at the front of the body with the bright side facing forward, or toward you. Leave just a tiny bit of the bare quill exposed.

19. Wrap the feather with the bright side of the feather facing forward—that is, as the leading edge. This helps prevent the barbs from leaning forward. Wrap to the rear of the wing, with each turn abutting the previous one. The quill will naturally seat itself, so don't leave spaces between the turns of hackle.

21. Wrap forward in front of the wing again, and tie off the hackle feather a little short of the eye. When securing the feather, hold it straight up and make the thread wraps on top of the hook, so as to avoid clogging the eye. Trim all excess material, then make a whip finish.

20. Cross under the wings at the "thorax" spot, then take a couple of turns in front of the wing (1). Now we depart from standard procedure. Carefully wrap rearward, passing behind the wing and deploying some additional turns of hackle there (2). If you see these turns displacing the previous ones, back off, wiggle the quill a bit to reposition it, and continue wrapping.

22. The finished Up-Chuck.

High-quality dry-fly saddle hackle is much preferred for these generously hackled flies. Because of their fine, flexible quills, these remarkable hackles enable the use of a single feather. The method used here involves wrapping the feather forward to the front of the wing, then back through itself to behind the wing, then forward once more. This simulates the deployment of hackle that formerly required two or more feathers. Other hackling methods are used on more sparsely dressed flies, as will be shown. In fact, one can often dress several or more flies with one saddle feather.

Cree hackle is made up of grizzly-type barring with brown and/or ginger components. It is not a basic strain of chicken and is not predictable in breeding. This results in Cree being in short supply. If you don't happen to

This stuff for moistening one's fingers doubles as an excellent dubbing helper.

This pretty Irish brown trout went for the Up-Chuck.

have Cree or some similar barred, variant-type hackle, use two feathers: ginger or brown combined with grizzly, as you would with the conventional Adams.

Those of you who've read my ramblings in the past may recall that for many years, I've been extolling the virtues of nonstandard colors and markings in hackle. Until recently, it's been somewhat hard to find, the reason being that most fly shops prefer to stock standard colors, as specified in the pattern books.

Recently, a supplier of fly-tying materials in New Jersey started dealing in unusual shades of hackle. The proprietor, John Snively, calls his operation, aptly, Fly Tyer Variant. His website is www.flytyervariant.com. Each cape or saddle is shown individually and has a code number. Thus, when you place an order, you get the *same exact pelt* that you saw on the web page. Kudos to John.

I've borrowed something from Francis Betters's excellent pattern, the Ausable Wulff: the use of hot orange thread. This blends with the body material to create an alluring effect, especially once the fly gets a little damp. I like to use liquid floatant, rather than paste, as this brings out this effect to its fullest. If you want a more subdued fly, use brown thread.

Even though the Up-Chuck is tied fairly large, getting the dubbing material to pack neatly is desirable. I am not a lover of sticky waxes; I find that they create more problems than they solve. However, a bit of smooth, not-very-sticky wax can be helpful. The stuff sold in office supply stores that helps people sort papers works great. I use SORTKWIK from Staples, but so far as I can tell, they are all pretty much the same.

About the Up-Chuck in action. I was fishing the streams of the lovely Boyne Valley in Ireland with Mr. Peter O'Reilly, a superior angler and most gracious host. The water was higher than we would have preferred, and we were relegated to fishing the smaller feeder streams. After trying several methods and patterns with only moderate success, I tied on a size 12 Up-Chuck with a Pheasant Tail Nymph dropper hanging down several feet.

Peter approved of my nymphing tactic but told me not to expect any results from the Up-Chuck. I explained that the large dry fly was there only as a strike indicator. But to the amazement of both of us, the wild Irish browns went for the dry almost to the exclusion of the nymph! After several of these exquisitely beautiful trout had been brought to hand and released, Peter asked if he might have a closer look at this "Oop-Chuck." Of course, I shared. Later in the week, he compensated by giving me an Irish pattern called the Murrough, which caught me a four-pond brown trout on Lough Sheelin.

Wood Duck Wings and Stripped Quill Bodies

The Cahill Quill has accounted for many thousands of fine trout over the years and is still an effective and enduring pattern.

IN THIS CHAPTER YOU'LL LEARN
1. The wood duck wing.
2. The spread tail, and a type of feather that works very well for dry-fly tails.
3. The stripped-hackle quill body, and how it can be altered in color.
4. The two-feather hackling method.

EXPLANATIONS
Q. Why the wood duck wing?

A. This material makes a wing that is air-resistant enough to help land the fly upright, but not so much so as to twist the leader. Also, it suggests the markings, or pattern, on certain mayfly wings.

Q. Why the spread tail?

A. A well-spread tail becomes a snowshoe. A bunched tail becomes a wick that sucks up water.

Q. Why the quill body?

A. The lighter-darker segmentations yield a realistic appearance. Also, the body is light and doesn't absorb water.

Q. Why use two cape feathers for the hackle?

A. Cape feathers have much shorter "sweet spots," meaning the area of prime hackle, than saddle feathers. They also tend to have a lower barb count—that is, barbs per inch of quill. This means that two feathers may be needed to deploy a sufficient amount of hackle, except on smaller flies.

A comment on that last statement. As generic hackle continues to evolve, capes are becoming more like saddles, with longer usable portions of the feathers and higher barb counts. This is worth noting for future hackle purchases.

The lemon-barred wood duck flank feather wing is found on many time-proven patterns; likewise, the quill body. I have good news and bad news. The good is that this wing is tied in the same manner as the hairwing of the Up-Chuck. The bad is that wood duck is rather pricey. Therefore, it's important to understand how to utilize all or most of the feathers, both large and small.

Essentially, there are three methods for tying this wing:

1. Sections taken from each side of a centered feather or from two opposing feathers.
   Advantages: Light and delicate, creates minimal bulk at the tie-in point, no need to deal with quill.
   Disadvantages: Requires prime feathers, sometimes two. Somewhat time-consuming.

2. Both wings formed from one large, centered feather.
   Advantages: Easy to tie, good-looking. May be able to use leftover portion of a centered feather.
   Disadvantages: Requires at least a semiprime feather, creates some bulk at the tie-in point, must deal with quill at the tip end.

3. Wings formed from two small feathers.
   Advantages: Produces excellent shape and silhouette, utilizes smaller feathers that would otherwise go to waste.
   Disadvantages: The two quills create bulk at the tie-in point.

Because wood duck is a little pricey, why waste any of it that's usable? Note that the remaining part of a feather that has been used in methods 1 or 2 can be used by itself if sufficient to form a wing, or if not, two such pieces can be used together.

Method 1: Sections can be taken from each side of a centered feather or from the "good" sides of two opposing feathers (a left and a right) that have usable material on only one side of the quill.

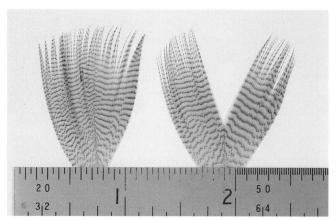

Method 2: Both wings can be formed from the centermost barbs of one large feather where the quill runs down the middle, or nearly so. It may be necessary to notch out a bit of the quill, so that it doesn't become part of the wings on one side or the other.

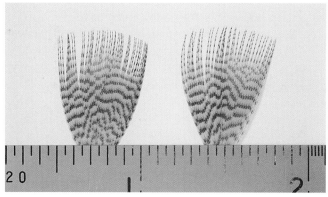

Method 3: Wings can be formed from two small feathers tied back-to-back, meaning with the convex sides curving away from each other.

The "leftovers" from methods 1 and 2 can be used, either singly or in pairs, to make wings.

The following tying sequence shows how to tie the wings with two back-to-back sections, method 1 above. The other methods will be shown in subsequent chapters, including an example of how the disadvantage of bulk at the tie-in point can be converted into an asset in body shaping.

HACKLE QUILLS FOR BODIES

Quill bodies are good-looking and lightweight, and they yield a realistic segmented effect. When I began tying, there were three predominant materials for making quill bodies: peacock, hackle quill, and condor. The third has been illegal for a long time, and justifiably so. There's also light and dark moose mane; we'll leave that until later.

Stripped-hackle quills are cheap and easy to use. Actually, they may be a freebie, as they can be taken from the large feathers at the rear of your dry-fly capes, thereby extending their utility.

A nice Beaverkill trout fooled by the Cahill Quill.

All quills, the stripped-hackle ones in particular, can be rather brittle. The best way I've found to soften them is by storing them in a mixture of water and hair conditioner. One part conditioner to five parts water is about right. You can put them in the mixture in a small jar and leave them there indefinitely—for a year or more, in fact.

Softening quills in this manner also enables you to flatten them, which makes them easier to wrap. This also enhances their appearance by widening them, so that the resulting segmentations more closely resemble those of the real insects. Simply lay them out and rub them with any smooth, cylindrical object, such as a ballpoint pen. There's also an item available in fly shops called a burnishing tool that does a superb job of flattening quills. It's made by Gudebrod and costs only a few dollars.

QUICK AND EASY DYE JOBS FOR QUILLS

Sometimes it's desirable to enhance or alter the color of hackle quills. A quick and easy method for dyeing quills is with, would you believe, unsweetened Kool-Aid! I use the small packets that make two quarts of the drink. However, I mix it very thick, using only enough water to form a viscous mixture. I add the water a little at a time, using an eyedropper. If needed, more water can be added, but only a drop or two at a time.

For years, I tinted quills with permanent markers, and that was okay. However, I've found that the Kool-Aid method yields truer colors, and as an added benefit, it does not interact with the thinners in protective coatings, especially cyanoacrylate adhesives, such as Zap-A-Gap. Some marker colors do very strange things when Zap-A-Gap is applied.

The process doesn't take long, just an hour or so. When you take the quills out of the Kool-Aid and dry them with a paper towel, they're ready for use. The colors are amazingly durable. When I first tried this method, I soaked some dyed quills in water overnight, and the next morning, I couldn't remove the dye, even by rubbing. It gives one pause for thought about what we're putting in our kids' stomachs.

There are six colors I've found useful: red (cherry), green (lemon-lime), orange, purple (grape), yellow (lemonade), and blue (berry blue). The packets are of the color that the enclosed Kool-Aid will yield. The purple grape turns a medium brown quill into a great shade for *Isonychia bicolor*, the large mahogany dun. I bet Jim Jones and his followers didn't know that.

You can also mix colors. Red and purple make maroon or claret, blue and green with orange mixed in make olive, and so on. Keep in mind that the basic color of the quill affects the resulting shade. Use paler quills in light-colored dye baths.

From the top, left to right: Ginger hackle quill dyed yellow, white hackle quill dyed yellow, brown hackle quill dyed yellow. White hackle quill dyed claret, white hackle quill dyed red, white hackle quill dyed purple. Ginger hackle quill dyed orange, cream hackle quill dyed green/olive, peacock quill dyed yellow/olive.

This is such a convenient method of dyeing! You don't have to deal with harsh chemicals or hot water. This being a cold-dye process, no damage is done to the quills by cooking them. Cleanup is a snap; all you need is water.

A large number of quills can be dyed at one time. However, I would suggest that once you've used the dye batch, you dispose of it. I tried using some that I'd saved for a few days, and the color I got wasn't the same as when the dye was fresh. At 25 cents a package, the Kool-Aid should be well within any budget.

In any case, the quills must be protected with a coating. A superglue, such as Zap-A-Gap or Plastic Surgery, works great. In lieu of that, two coats of clear head cement is okay, and a water-based lacquer is even better. Be sure the quills have dried thoroughly before applying any of these coatings.

THE CAHILL QUILL

Hook:	Dry fly; here, a Daiichi model 1180.
Thread:	Tan or medium brown 8/0 Uni-Thread or comparable.
Wings:	Lemon-barred wood duck; two opposing sections laid back-to-back.
Tail:	Ginger hackle barbs.
Body:	Ginger or brown hackle quill, stripped.
Hackle:	Two cape feathers, straw cream or light ginger.

Here, I've used a quill dyed pale orange with Kool-Aid to illustrate the sort of color that results from this dyeing method. Notice that the quill doesn't come out a bright orange, but rather a soft, natural-looking shade.

If you wish to tie a variation of the Cahill Quill, use barred ginger hackle or mix in a grizzly for the second hackle. Trout seem to like that.

1. Tie on and form a thread base, as you did for the Up-Chuck. We're using winging method 1, so prepare the two sections of wood duck. They should look like those in the photo, viewed from the top.

2. Measure the sections against the hook shank. They should be about equal to it in length.

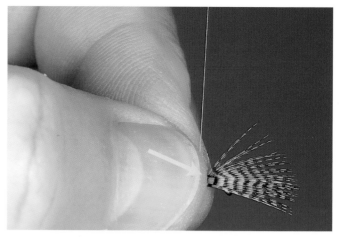

3. Position the wood duck on the thread base, and tie it on with a few pinch wraps. A pinch wrap is done by bringing the thread straight up; capturing it, the winging fibers, and the hook shank tightly between the thumb and forefinger; then bringing the thread down the far side of the hook, sneaking it back between the fingers, and pulling straight downward. This keeps the winging material on top of the hook, where it belongs. Repeat the pinch wrap several times, being careful not to disturb the diverging curvature.

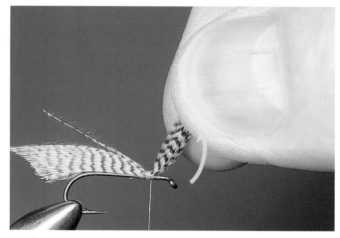

4. If you feel that the wing fibers are fairly well secured, take a few wraps behind the wing. Then, before locking the wood duck down completely, stroke the fibers upward to be sure they are all precisely on top of the hook and have not been carried by thread torque to the far side.

5. Slope-cut the wing butts.

6. Bind them down, forming a smooth, tapered foundation. This is even more important than it was with the Up-Chuck, because the quill body won't hide any lumpiness.

7. Stand up the wood duck fibers per the instructions for standing up a hair bunch in the previous chapter; you'll find that fewer thread wraps are required. Then divide the fibers into two equal wings by locating and reestablishing the original convex-to-convex curvature.

8. Form the wings with **X**-wraps and figure eights, following the instructions for the hairwing on the Up-Chuck. The arrow shows the taper of the underbody.

9. How the wing should look from the front.

10. This femoral tract feather has long, stiff barbs, ideal for dry-fly tailing.

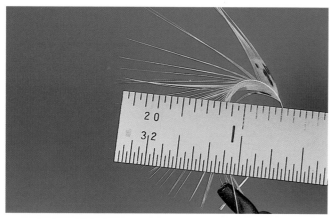

11. The length of the barbs.

12. Select a bunch of tailing barbs by stroking them out at 90 degrees from the quill, so that the tips are more or less even. Then slope-cut the butts and lay them on top of the slope-cut wing butts. Tie them in place with pinch wraps, then smoothly bind them down with thread, working up toward the rear of the wings, then back to the rear, so as to further shape and smooth out the underbody.

13. A few turns of thread under the tail fibers help spread the tail.

14. Tie in the body quill by the tip and bind it down to complete the shaping of the underbody.

15. Wrap the quill forward with each turn abutting the one before, and tie it off well short of the wings.

16. Select two cape feathers of proper size, and strip them back to the sweet spots. "Spoon" the feathers, and tie them in together beneath the hook in the front of the quill body, pretty sides forward. *Important*: Leave just a bit of bare quill exposed at the tie-in point, so that the quills

are able to rotate into position before any barbs begin to deploy. Move the thread ahead of the wings, further securing the quill butts. Cut off the excess, and smooth out the area with thread, in preparation for wrapping the hackle.

17. Probably one of the feathers will tell you (visibly) that it wants to be first. Wrap this feather up to the rear of the wing, each turn abutting the one before. Then cross over underneath the wings and continue in front. Tie off the feather well short of the eye, and neatly trim the quill and any errant fibers.

18. Wrap the second hackle through the first one. You'll discover that the quill finds the little niches and seats itself readily. If you should notice any disturbance or displacement of fibers from the first hackle, back off a turn or two and rewrap.

19. As before, pass the second feather under the wings, and make however many wraps forward of the wings that can be done without crowding the eye. Again, neaten up with careful trimming, then finish the fly with a whip finish.

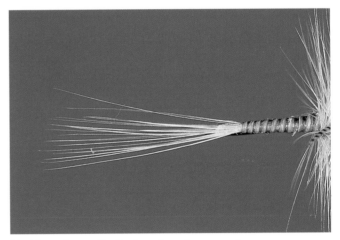

20. Top view of tail, showing the spread.

Having mentioned Zap-A-Gap, here's how to handle the stuff. First, the container is opened by breaking off the cap from the end of the tube. The opening is quite narrow, which causes the glue to remain in the tube itself, rather than run down into the bottle. Cutting back the end of the tube a bit solves this problem. The photos and captions convey some other helpful suggestions for dealing with this volatile adhesive.

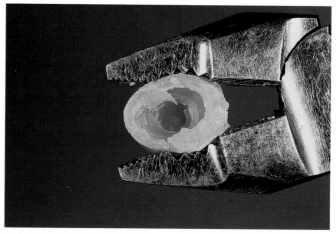

If the cap becomes encrusted, squeeze it with pliers, which will loosen the dried glue and enable its removal.

Zap-A-Gap comes with the cap joined to the bottle. To open it, break the cap from the tube.

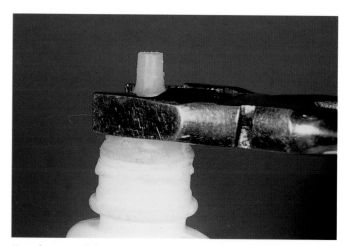

Dried material from around the tube can be removed in the same manner.

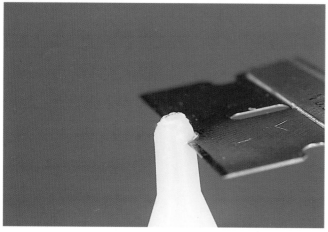

Increase the inside diameter of the tube by cutting off the top ¹/₈ inch. The cap still fits.

It's much easier to keep track of the cap if it's painted some bright color.

More Wood Duck Wings and Peacock Quill Bodies

5

IN THIS CHAPTER YOU'LL LEARN
1. Stripping peacock quills.
2. Dyeing peacock quills.

I believe the reasons for using peacock quills for bodies will be self-evident as this chapter progresses, so I'll omit the explanations. For those tiers who have not previously used peacock quills, a few notes about their nature and how to prepare them are in order.

The quills taken from the eye of the feather are light on one edge and dark on the other. This makes for a most attractive segmented appearance. To obtain the best light-dark effect, tie in and wrap the quill with the dark edge to the rear. It's preferable to tie them in by the tip end, in order to take advantage of the slightly tapered shape of the quill.

Note that the dark edge of the quill is that to which the herl, or fuzz, adheres. With the "pretty" side of the eye facing you, the quills on the right of the main stem better accommodate being tied in by the tip with the dark edge to the rear. Those taken from the left side must be tied in back-side-facing, which may produce slightly less contrast. If this bothers you, simply tie in the lefties by the butt end, and overlap the wraps slightly to create the well-spaced segmentation.

STRIPPING PEACOCK QUILLS
Quills from the main stem surrender their herl easily; it can be scraped off with a thumbnail. However, they do not have the light-dark contrast. Those from the eye are more resistant in surrendering herl. I've found that those that have been lying around for a long time may relinquish their herl to the thumbnail method, so you should try that first. However, in most cases, a more assiduous method is required. It's a bit of a chore—but worth the effort.

Stripping with an Eraser
Rubbing off the fuzz with an eraser yields the best results, especially using a pencil-type eraser. The abrasive rubber composite found on double-ended erasers also works very well. Simply lay out the quill on a piece of cardboard and rub away.

As a rule of thumb, the larger the eye of the feather, the longer, stronger, wider, and better-marked the quill. When selecting peacock feathers for quilling, squeeze the eyed area and observe the back side. The lighter the quills flash, the better the contrast.

Stripping with Clorox
Entire eyes can be stripped with Clorox, but it's a procedure fraught with peril. If you wish to give it a try, pour some Clorox into a small soup dish and add a little water to slow it down a bit. Have ready another bowl containing a stop bath of water mixed with baking soda.

Swish the eye around; you'll see the Clorox taking on a tealike color as the fuzz is removed. The *instant* that the last bit of fuzz disappears, dunk the eye into the stop bath. With luck, the light-dark markings are still present, and the quills haven't been eaten away to the point where they are useless.

Let the eye dry; then soak it for a little while in a mixture of 20 percent hair conditioner and 80 percent water. This will help soften the material and make it easier to wrap without splitting. However, don't store the quills in the mixture, as was suggested with hackle quills, and let them dry before using them.

One good thing about the Clorox method is that the eyes thus stripped can be dyed whole—that is, without removing the individual quills from the main stem.

DYEING PEACOCK QUILLS
As with hackle quills, Kool-Aid dyes can be used to color peacock quills. For the Red Quill, I've used a quill from a peacock eye dyed with orange Kool-Aid. This is a departure from the original dressing, which specified a stripped brown hackle quill. Notice how the light-dark contrast of the peacock quill is maintained.

Both stripped peacock and hackle quills, dyed several useful colors, are available in fly shops. These are very handy. However, I've found the peacock quills to be quite delicate, apparently the result of the stripping process. The hair conditioner and water treatment will soften them, but they still require very careful handling.

THE RED QUILL

The wing on the Red Quill utilizes the second wood duck winging method: a single feather, bunched and divided. It may be necessary to snip out the center quill from such feathers, but only if it is prominent, and only that portion that would affect the formation of the wing.

The dressing for the Red Quill:

Hook:	Dry fly; here, a Daiichi model 1180.
Thread:	Medium brown 8/0 Uni-Thread or comparable.
Wings:	Wood duck, as described.
Tail:	Gray hackle barbs or Micro Fibetts; here, the hackle barbs.
Body:	Orange-dyed peacock quill.
Hackle:	Medium gray; here, a single saddle feather.

On larger hook sizes, even a prime peacock quill might not be long enough to cover the body. In such a case, use two quills. You have several options:

1. Tie both of the quills in at the rear, spiral-wrap the first one, then wrap the second one in the gaps between the wraps of the first one. This takes a bit of practice.
2. Tie in both of the quills at the rear, and wrap them both at once. This takes a *lot* of practice.
3. Tie in one of the quills by the tip at the rear, wrap it as far as it will reach, and tie it off. Then tie in another one by the butt and finish the body.

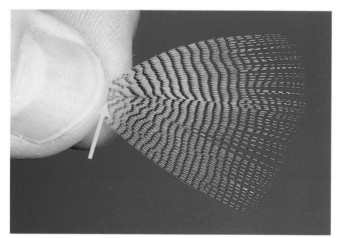

1. Hold the wood duck feather by the "delta"—that is, the spot where the quill and the fibers come together—not just by the quill alone.

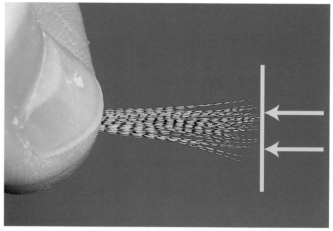

2. Compress the fibers into a bunch. You'll probably find that you need to stroke them toward the tips at a slight angle, in order to compensate for the differences in length, so that the tip ends come out as even as possible.

3. Form the wing and tie on the tail, following the instructions for the Cahill Quill. Then tie in the orange-dyed peacock quill by either the tip or the butt, in such a manner as to allow the dark edge to be the trailing edge when wrapped.

4. Wrap the quill edge-to-edge, and tie it off rearward of the wing.

5. Coat the quill body with adhesive, either now or after the fly is finished.

6. Here, I am using a single saddle feather, which, because of its quality attributes, will adequately dress this type of dry fly, with feather to spare. Prepare the feather by stripping the quill until quality barbs are reached. Tie in the hackle feather as per previous instructions, bright side facing forward and a tiny bit of the bare quill exposed. Wrap it back-to-front, bright side forward, each wrap abutting the previous one and passing underneath the wing at the thorax spot. Tie off the feather on top of the hook, thus clearing the eye, and make a whip-finish.

7. The finished Red Quill.

THE QUILL GORDON

The Quill Gordon uses the third wood duck winging method. The wing is formed out of two small wood duck feathers, tied convex-to-convex, so that they flare away from each other. Notice how the butts are slope-cut to form a filled-out, nicely tapered underbody.

The dressing for the Quill Gordon:

Hook:	Daiichi model 1180 or similar.
Thread:	Beige or tan 8/0 Uni-Thread or comparable.
Wings:	Wood duck, as described.
Tail:	Gray hackle barbs or Micro Fibetts; here, the latter.
Body:	Two natural peacock quills.
Hackle:	Gray; here, a dun variant saddle feather.

1. Two small wood duck feathers, held back-to-back so that they flare away from each other.

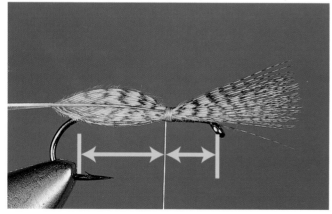

2. The feathers tied in. Use firm pinch wraps, so that their position is maintained and secured.

3. Slope-cut the wing feather butts and neatly bind them down, forming a nicely tapered underbody. Then wrap forward and complete the wings, following the instructions for methods 1 and 2, previously shown. Then wrap to the rear.

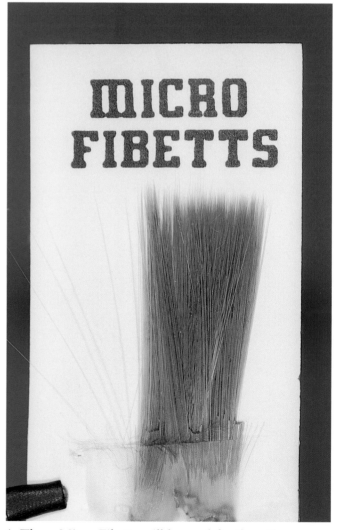

4. These Micro Fibetts will be used for the tail.

5. Tie on the tail fibers, and jam a few turns of thread under them at the tie-in point, so as to spread them.

8. Wrap the second quill as a continuation of the body, and tie it off just rearward of the wings.

6. Tie in the first peacock quill, dark edge to the rear, and wrap it as shown. Use it up, then tie it off.

9. If you wish, make the hackle with the simple, straightforward method used for the Red Quill. However, if you'd like to try a useful option that will yield a slightly more dense hackle, tie in a saddle feather on top of the hook, about halfway between the eye of the hook and the front of the wing, as shown.

7. Tie in the second quill. Try to make the spot where the two quills join as inconspicuous as possible.

10. Start the turns in front of the wing, working rearward. Cross under the wing and wrap back to the front of the body.

11. Complete the fly by wrapping forward, crossing under the wing again, tying off, neatly trimming all excess, and making a whip finish.

The Flat-Hackled Parachutes

6

IN THIS CHAPTER YOU'LL LEARN

1. The hair wing post for parachutes.
2. Several body options.
3. Several unique patterns that represent different forms of stream insects.
4. The single-feather parachute hackling method.
5. An alternative to tying off the hackle and whip-finishing the head of the fly.

EXPLANATIONS

Q. Why tie in the hair post material tips-first?
A. This helps shape the body of the fly.

Q. Why wrap the hackle counterclockwise, looking down from the top?
A. Because this avoids doubling the quill back on itself, and it also results in the hackle and tying thread being wrapped in the same direction.

Q. Why the Zap-A-Gap finishing technique?
A. Because tying off parachute hackle and executing a whip finish is difficult on parachutes.

Q. Why trim the wing post?
A. Because it is only there to hold the hackle and make the fly visible to the angler. It's not intended to be a realistic representation of actual wings.

Q. Why the preference for prime dry-fly saddle feathers?
A. To minimize quill thickness and maximize barb count, thereby enabling single-feather hackling.

Q. Why tie in and wrap the hackle with the dull side down?
A. The feathers tend to lean a bit toward the dull side, as they are slightly concave. This helps keep the hackle from riding up the wing post.

My mentor with regard to parachute-style flies was the inimitable Dudley G. "Dud" Soper. Dud walked to the beat of a very different drum, and that included his preference for flies. But he was no "Dud" when it came to deceiving trout that were playing hard-to-get. His weapon of choice was the parachute-hackled fly. Dud's flies were rough—both in appearance and with respect to their effect on trout. He preferred to fish challenging waters—calm, quiet pools where the trout calibrated one's tippet—and was truly a master in such intimidating environs.

Parachute flies have come into more widespread use in recent years, anglers having discovered how effective they can be. In the spring of 1999, I was treated to a refresher course in Parachutes 401 on a stream in Pennsylvania's Poconos. During a heavy caddis hatch, a friend with whom I was sharing a pool outfished me four to one. After darkness drove us off the water, he showed me the fly that had done the job. It was called a Klinkhamer. I think it's an ideal pattern with which to demo a few tricks in tying the flat hackle.

Sim Savage with a Klinkhamer-addicted rainbow trout.

A few compromises are acceptable with reference to the quality of parachute hackle. It doesn't have to be absolutely the stiffest and strongest—and the most expensive—on the market. However, two characteristics are very important: a very thin, flexible quill and a high barb count. The latter facilitates applying an adequate amount of hackle with a minimal number of turns, which is critical in parachute tying. Either cape or saddle may be used, provided the feather meets the stated criteria.

THE TYPICAL KLINKHAMER

Here's a typical Klinkhamer dressing. Note that a uniquely shaped hook is required for tying proper Klinks.

Hook:	A light-wire scud hook; here, the Daiichi model 1130.
Thread:	Brown 8/0 Uni-Thread or comparable.
Wing post:	White hair: calf tail or body hair, fine bucktail, whatever.
Body:	Bright green dubbing.
Collar: (optional)	Peacock herl or black dubbing.
Hackle:	Light brown or barred ginger saddle; here, the latter.

The most vexing problem tiers encounter on parachutes is tying off. There's another option, that being the use of superglue, as shown in the following tying sequence.

1. Wrap a thread base in this position.

2. Stack the tips of a small bunch of hair, and tie it in by the tips, thus forming the wing post and tapering the underbody in one operation.

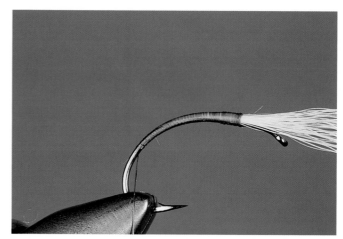

3. Wrap neatly to the rear, well around the bend.

4. Spin on the dubbing of your choice and form the body, stopping just short of the wing post. Stand up the wing post with thread wraps tight to the front of the hair.

5. Tie in the peacock herl at the front of the body, then advance the thread to the front of the wing post.

6. Wrap the herl to form a thorax, tie it off, and trim the excess.

7. This type of feather makes good parachute hackle: It has a high barb count and very fine quill.

8. Tie in the hackle feather on the top of the hook, *dull-side-down*, with the tip hanging off to the rear. Be sure to leave some bare quill exposed. Hold the feather straight up, lay the quill in with the wing-post hair, and form a base by wrapping the thread around the base of the hair and the quill. Wrap counterclockwise, looking down from the top. Left-handed tiers wrap clockwise.

9. Wrap the feather *dull-side-down*, counterclockwise if you're right-handed. The second wrap should go beneath the first one. Continue to wrap under very gentle tension.

10. Gently lift the hackle, tie down the feather, and trim the excess. Then make a whip finish.

12. The finished fly, side view.

11. Lock in the hackle by applying a very small droplet of Zap-A-Gap at the center of the hackle wraps. After it has dried, cut the wing post to the desired length.

13. The finished fly, top view.

THE KLINKHAMER AS A MAYFLY EMERGER

While the Klink was designed to be a caddis emerger, it also serves very well as a mayfly emerger. Here's a pattern designed to simulate a typical mayfly struggling to escape from its nymphal shuck. The body and hackle colors are intended to imitate a number of the important *Ephemerella* and *Drunella* mayflies that are commonly found in trout waters across America. For the blue-winged olives of the *Drunella* genus, you might use pheasant tail dyed olive for the body. Sizes range from little 18s for *Ephemerella dorothea* to 8s and 10s for the large *Drunella grandis*, commonly called the western green drake.

Hook:	The same; a Daiichi model 1130 or similar.
Thread:	Brown 8/0 Uni-Thread or comparable.
Wing post:	Hair as specified for the typical Klink.
Tail:	A few pheasant tail fibers.
Body:	Pheasant tail fibers, wrapped.
Ribbing: (optional)	Very fine copper wire or rust-colored thread, reverse-wrapped.
Hackle:	Medium gray.
Adhesive:	Zap-A-Gap or similar.

Here you'll see a much easier method of securing the hackle on a parachute. It eliminates a difficult process and possibly upsetting that beautiful hackle you just wrapped.

1. Tie in the wing-post hair as per the Klinkhamer instructions. Then temporarily reposition the hook in the vise as shown, and tie on a small bunch of pheasant tail fibers and the ribbing wire.

2. Restore the hook to its former position, wrap the pheasant fibers to form the body, secure them, and trim. Then reverse-wrap the ribbing wire—that is, wrap it toward you instead of away from you, as shown by the arrow, so that each wrap crosses the pheasant herl. Secure it, and cut off the excess.

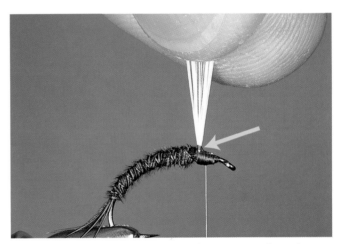

3. Tie in the hackle as previously instructed, and wrap the quill in with the post hair. It's not visible in the photo, but trust me—it's in with the hair.

4. Wrap the hackle as instructed in the Klink exercise. Then grab the hackle and the tying thread with a pair of fairly heavy hackle pliers, make sure the quill and thread are together, and let it all hang down.

6. After the adhesive has thoroughly dried, simply cut off the excess feather. No tie-offs, no whip-finish knots to disturb the hackle.

5. Apply a generous drop of Zap-A-Gap underneath the hook at the thorax location, working it into the quill, the thread, and the body. It's helpful to rotate the vise a bit, so that the hackle and thread make contact with the underside of the body.

7. Cutting the wing post to the desired length completes the fly.

THE KLINKHAMER AS A MIDGE EMERGER

While on the subject of the Klinkhamer design, let's look at how it might work as an emerging midge pattern. First, let's not confuse the name with diminution; not all midges are midgets. They are members of the order Diptera, the most prolific in the insect kingdom. True, some are tiny, almost microscopic. But others are huge. There are giant craneflies whose legs span a tea saucer!

There are times when midges can be very important. I well remember a wintry late September morning when a midge emergence saved my day on Armstrong's Spring Creek. I got up at 7:00 A.M. and looked out of the motel window at almost a foot of fresh snow. Having paid for my day in advance, I grabbed a coffee and donut and went out to the stream. At 8:00 A.M., it looked like a subarctic wasteland.

I drove back into Livingston and enjoyed a proper breakfast. By 9:00, one of the fly shops had opened, and I went in to commiserate with the guys who worked there. They told me that I'd better get back out to the creek and check out what was happening.

I did so, and to my amazement, trout were rising all over the place. A midge hatch was in progress, and the fish were feasting on the emerging larvae. I didn't have a good pattern, actually, but a soft-hackle wet fly fished in the surface film took enough trout to keep me happy.

Here's a midge emerger pattern I like. It can—and should—be tied in a variety of colors and sizes, predicated on what the midges look like in the waters you fish. This information is not easily obtained, as midges have not been given the exposure that mayflies, caddisflies, and stoneflies have received. You'll have to rely on your powers of observation—and seining the surface film during a hatch can be most beneficial.

Hook:	The same; a Daiichi model 1130 or similar.
Thread:	Brown 8/0 Uni-Thread or comparable.
Wing post:	Bright-colored hair: calf tail or body hair, fine bucktail, whatever.
Tail:	Chickabou or fine marabou, very short.
Body:	Synthetic stranded material; here, midge Larva Lace.
Hackle:	Light brown or ginger saddle, undersize.

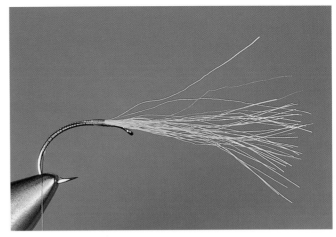

1. The post hair tied in.

2. Tie in the tail material here, just to the rear of the wing post. Measure the material against the rear of the hook to establish the length of the tail.

3. Wrap over the tail material, well down around the bend. This forms the tail and the underbody.

4. Wrap back to the wing-post location, and tie in the body material.

5. With the tying thread, bury the body material, wrapping all the way back to where the tail departs, then back to the wing-post location.

6. Wrap the body, tie it off, and cut off the excess material.

7. Follow the hackling and Zap-A-Gap procedures described previously.

8. The completed fly.

I should mention that Larva Lace offers some excellent synthetic materials. Visit their website: www.larvalace.com.

In the next chapter, you'll see a wing post made of a different material: closed-cell foam. You might want to incorporate this post on the Midge Larva Klink, as the synthetic body wrap doesn't have good flotation.

A Foam-Post Parachute

7

IN THIS CHAPTER, YOU'LL LEARN

1. An alternative wing post material
2. How the Zap-A Gap method makes it much easier to finish off a mixed two-feather hackle.

Here's another parachute pattern that I've fished with telling effect. I've named it the Monitor, after that Civil War ship that rode so low in the water. I suppose that, living in Manchester, New Hampshire, I should design a pattern called the Merrimack, after the river that flows through the middle of town. I'll work on it.

A handsome rainbow caught on the Monitor.

This fly is tied using a white closed-cell foam cylinder for the post. It not only abets visibility and flotation, it also makes tying the hackle quite easy. There are various types of foam on the market. My favorite for this operation is the die-cut cylindrical type from a company named Flycraft. Actually, these are ant bodies. They come precut in block form, in either white or black. Several sizes are available.

Flycraft offers a number of very useful foam products, including ant and beetle bodies, grasshopper and frog bodies, inchworm and damselfly bodies, and popper bodies. It isn't widely distributed in fly shops, at least not at this writing. These products can be obtained over the web at www.flycraft.com.

THE MONITOR

This Monitor pattern is actually a foam-post version of the highly potent Parachute Adams. Here's the dressing:

Hook:	Dry fly; the Daiichi model 1180 or similar.
Thread:	Black 8/0 Uni-Thread or comparable.
Wing post:	White foam cylinder, as described.
Tail (optional):	Cree if you have it, or brown and grizzly mixed, or either color alone.
Body:	Gray dubbing.
Hackle:	Brown and grizzly, mixed.

1. A closed-cell ant body cylinder from Flycraft.

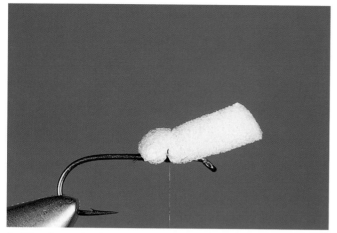

2. Tie the cylinder on top of the hook.

3. Stand the cylinder upright, and bury the tied-in part with thread.

4. Tie the tail and spin on the dubbing.

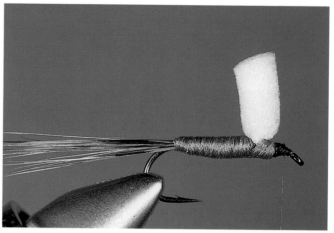

5. Wrap the body and take a turn or two ahead of the post, thus forming a thorax, and evening up the plane front and back of the wing post.

6. Tie in the two hackle feathers ahead of the wing post, dull-sides-down, with a bit of quill exposed. Hold them up straight, and take a half dozen or so counterclockwise (clockwise for lefties) wraps around the quills and the post.

7. Wrap the hackles both at the same time. You may find that this goes better if done by hand without hackle pliers, so that even tension is maintained on both feathers.

8. When finished, attach a pair of hackle pliers, catching the thread and the quills. Let everything hang down, then apply the Zap-A-Gap. Since the foam wing post isn't absorbent, you can apply adhesive around the base, as shown. After the adhesive has dried, cut off the feathers and thread beneath the hook. Cut the post to the desired length.

9. The finished fly, side view.

10. Top view.

The benefits of the Zap-A-Gap tie-off (glue-off?) multiply by a couple orders of magnitude here, because two hackles are being used. They are to be wrapped both at once. It's very helpful to wrap them with your fingers, rather than hackle pliers, if they are of sufficient length, so that they are in sync with each other. It's sort of like the principle of the differential, which enables an automobile to turn a corner. This is yet another advantage of using saddle hackles.

If you decide that you like the foam post, feel free to substitute it on the Klinkhamers and other parachute patterns.

The Parachute As A Spinner

IN THIS CHAPTER, YOU'LL LEARN

1. An easy way to make the egg sac that's so prominent on certain female spinners.
2. A different type of tail that's suggestive of that of a spent fly.

In the spring of 2001, I was invited to fish club waters on a northeastern Pennsylvania stream. I was not familiar with the hatch cycles there. I arrived on April 29 in time for the evening fishing. Nothing much happened until around 7:30. Then, suddenly, there were lots of spinners in the air, distinguished by their prominent yellow egg sacs, and the fish were taking them like jelly beans. *Ephemerella subvaria*—true Hendricksons! It was reminiscent of the good old times.

This fish was taken on the E-Foam-Erella during a Hendrickson spinner fall.

I had some spinners with me, and between those and an Adams Parachute, I did okay, but I felt that with a more imitative pattern, I'd have done much better. So, back at the lodge, I got out my tying kit and threw together a pattern. It worked very well indeed.

E-FOAM-ERELLA SPINNER

Hook:	Daiichi model 1180 dry fly, or model 1560 1XL light-wire nymph.
Thread:	Brown 8/0 Uni-Thread or similar.
Wing post:	White hair, either natural or synthetic.
Egg sac:	Yellow closed-cell foam.
Tails (optional):	Thin hackle quills from a light gray or white cape or saddle.
Body:	Rust-colored dubbing.
Hackle:	Light gray or white, tied parachute-style, slightly oversize.

1. Stack the wing-post hair bunch, then tie it in by the tip end.

2. After standing up the hair, as described in the Klink-hamer instructions, wrap the thread to the rear and down around the bend a little.

3. Tie in the foam strip.

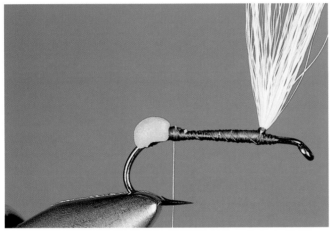

4. Fold the foam strip forward, tie it down, then trim the excess and bind down the little lump of foam that's left.

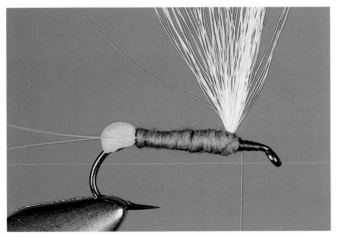

5. Tie in the tail fibers, one on each side of the hook, so that the foam egg sac spreads them. Then wrap the body.

6. Complete the fly by adding the hackle, following previous parachute hackle instructions.

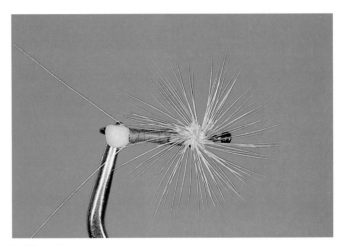

7. Top view.

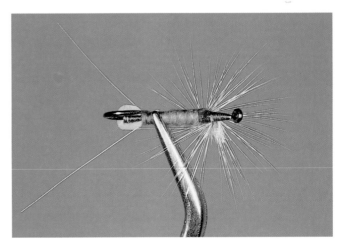

8. Bottom view.

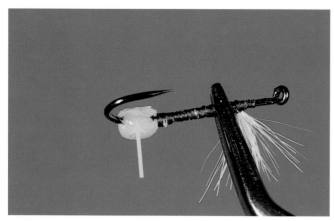

9. If having the thread show under the egg sac bothers you, touch it up with a little water-base acrylic paint.

You'll notice that the tying thread shows a little on the bottom of the egg sac. Based on my experiences with the effectiveness of this fly, I don't believe this matters one iota to the fish. However, if it offends you, I suggest one of two remedies: Either use yellow tying thread, or place a small drop of acrylic paint in the crevice, covering the wraps. I suggest that this be done immediately after making the egg sac, so as not to get paint on the tails or body. You can prepare a bunch of them in advance and set them aside to dry.

Continuing the E-Foam-Erella story: The next day was hot and sunny, not a cloud in the sky. We looked for Hendrickson duns in the late morning and throughout the afternoon. I don't recall seeing a single one riding the water in classic fashion; those that we did see were already airborne, and they came off sporadically all day and well into the evening. There was virtually no interest on the part of the trout, and we resorted to nymphing in order to move a few fish.

We hoped for a repeat of the spinner activity for the evening fishing. Finally they started, but quite late. I had parked myself at the head of a long, slow pool to watch for rises. I got there about 5:30 P.M. By 7:25, I had seen less than a dozen indifferent rises, and I was fishless. I was about to switch to a large indicator fly and a nymph dropper, when suddenly several rises came in quick succession, and there were the egg-laden spinners, zooming over the riffle coming into the pool. To make a long story short, by 8:20, when my friend came to collect me, I had hooked sixteen trout from 12 to 17 inches and had landed fifteen of them. In the fading light of evening, I was able to get away with a 5X tippet, and later 4X, and I brought the fish to net with dispatch.

We decided to get out a little earlier the next day, figuring that maybe, with the hot, clear weather, the spinners would be coming back in the morning. Turned out that we were right—more so than we had expected. We got on the stream at around 9:00 A.M., and the egg-laden imagoes were already hovering low over the water. We got into fish immediately, but a half hour later, it was over. We were too late.

The next day, we were onstream at 7:00 A.M. Lo and behold, there were the spinners! This time, we had over an hour of fast action. And so it went throughout the rest of the week. The thing that surprised me was that although we didn't see that many duns, the spinner flights were quite substantial. Obviously the lack of a concentrated emergence camouflaged the fact that duns were coming off in fair numbers.

The 1XL model 1560 hook mentioned above seems to work out a little better for the laying out of the components. It's listed as a nymph/wet-fly hook, but I've found that it's light enough for dry-fly work, given good-quality hackle.

I listed the tails as being optional. They do balance the fly nicely, as the egg sac spreads them wide. In Pennsylvania, the fish seemed to like them, or at least they didn't reject them. However, I fished a Hendrickson spinner fall on a New England river only a few days later, and I found that the trout there took the fly more willingly after I chopped off the tails. Why? Who knows? Just play it by ear.

I think there's a message or two here. First, our climate *does* seem to be changing, despite the scoffing heard from the contingent that would prefer to ignore this. Second, insects are amazingly adaptable even over a very short time span. We've seen this in other aspects of life, notably in the field of health, where viruses mutate quickly and constantly. It's a little scary. But what it means to us fly fishers is that we must hang loose, so to speak, and be ready to react to change as it occurs.

I feel that this experience with the Hendricksons can be projected to most, if not all, emergences on our trout waters today. I've been following the evolution of this phenomenon for several decades now, and there's no doubt in my mind that the alteration of the environment, and the extremes in weather that it has caused, has a profound effect on the behavior of the bugs. I well remember one very early spring following a virtual non-winter when the *subvaria* Hendricksons appeared on the main Delaware in early April. We saw march browns in late April and, unbelievably, green drakes in early May. For about a month, we had a bonanza. Then things caught up with us, and we had midsummer conditions in the Northeast from mid-May on into September. We did not have good hatches for a couple of years thereafter, and I think the low, warm water of that season was responsible.

An Unkempt Yet Effective Parachute

9

IN THIS CHAPTER YOU'LL LEARN

1. An interesting and unique method for making a parachute hackle.
2. How to lock the hackle in place using the quill butts.

This fly is not meant to be realistic—at least, not to the angler's eye. I offer it solely on the basis of its amazing effectiveness.

Up to now, the exercises in tying parachutes have focused, to a large extent, on making the hackle neat and flat. This one represents a rather radical departure from that discipline.

For many years, I fished with a guy from Albany, New York, named Bill Dorato. We lost Bill at age eighty-seven, he having survived, over a period of 75 years, countless cigarettes and a diet that consisted mainly of coffee and chain-store cold cuts. It had to be his wonderful good nature that turned nicotine, tar, and preservatives into essential amino acids.

Bill was a terrific fisherman. He was patient, observant, and creative. This last trait was evidenced in his fly tying. Bill's flies were not all that neat; in fact, they were rather unkempt. He liked them that way. Apparently, the trout did also, as they worked super-well, and still do.

THE WOODSTOCK PARACHUTE

The following pattern is a takeoff on one Bill called the Sofa Pillow. It bears no resemblance to an old western stonefly pattern that bears that name, and I doubt that Bill even knew about that one. Since he never wrote about or took credit for his unique ties, it really didn't matter.

I call my version the Woodstock because it looks to me like that Charles Schulz character from the "Peanuts" comic strip. Here's the basic dressing:

Hook:	Typical dry fly; Daiichi model 1180 or comparable.
Thread:	Beige or brown 8/0 Uni-Thread or similar.
Wing post:	The butts of the tail and hackle quills.
Tails:	Stripped grizzly cape hackle quills.
Body:	Cream-colored or beige dubbing.
Hackle:	Ginger or brown and grizzly, mixed.

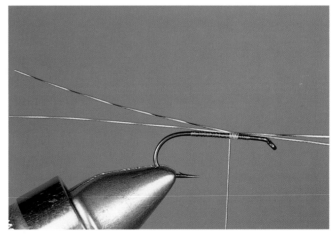

1. Tie in the stripped quills for the tail at the position where the hackle will be wrapped later. Don't cut off the butt ends; leave them long. Then wrap the thread to the bend.

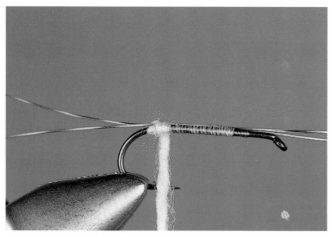

2. Spin on a little dubbing, and spread the tails by taking a crisscross wrap between the quills. The first turn goes over the hook, passing between the hook and quill on the far side. The second one passes beneath the hook, then up between it and the near-side quill. To see how this will look, refer to the last photo in this sequence.

3. With more dubbing, wrap the body and thorax, and in the process, stand up the quill butts.

4. Tie in the feathers as per previous parachute hackle instructions, leaving the quills long. Then stand them up and wrap thread around the base of all the quills, binding them into a single bunch.

5. Wrap all the hackles at once. As in the Monitor exercise, you may find that this goes better if done by hand without hackle pliers, so that even tension is maintained.

6. Bring the quills forward over the top, working them between the hackle barbs. You can cut a **V** out of the front of the hackle, if you wish. Lock in the hackle by tying off the quills.

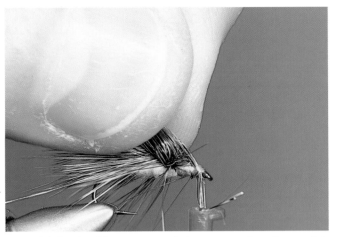

7. Hold the hackle up out of the way and make a whip finish.

8. A drop of Zap-A-Gap at the center secures and protects the hackle.

9. The finished fly, side view.

10. The finished fly, bottom view. Note how the tails are spread.

This fly works very well during the emergence of large, clumsy insects such as the march brown. It can be modified in color to suit the occasion. For example, you can use pale olive green for the body and mix in a hackle of similar color, and you have a Green Drake. Or use white for the body and plain grizzly for the hackle, and you have a Coffin Fly. Even so, I consider the Wood-stock fly to be more of a general, prospecting pattern, rather than an imitator.

Two Imitative Streamers

IN THIS CHAPTER YOU'LL LEARN

1. About some excellent feathers for making streamer flies.
2. Some insights on how to use them.
3. A method for attaching die-cut eyes and making them stay put.

I love catching landlocked salmon! The so-called landlock is, in actuality, an Atlantic salmon. They share the scientific name *Salmo salar*, "The Leaper." In this respect, the landlock equals, if not outdoes, its migratory brother. I've seen them jump so high that they were dry when they came down!

Here in the New England states, landlocks inhabit both rivers and lakes. The primordial strain sometimes produced fish well in excess of 10 pounds in weight, with a few topping 20. Not all that many years ago, such landlocks existed in the New England waters I fish. What I would give if they were here now!

Landlocks feed very much as trout do—that is, on the aquatic life indigenous to their habitat. They rise to hatch flies and are a blast to catch on drys. But the type of fly we'll look at here is a baitfish imitation—specifically, a smelt pattern.

The Winnie Boy accounted for this 4-pound landlocked salmon.

In springtime, around ice-out, when the freshwater smelt in the lakes school up and run into the feeder streams to spawn, the landlocks follow them. The water is still quite cold—and therefore, high in oxygen content—so the salmon remain close to the surface.

This is prime time. The landlocks are concentrated around the mouths of the brooks and are on the feed. In spite of this, they can be very capricious as to what sort of fly they're willing to take. Anglers have been trying to figure them out for many decades, yet seldom does a specific pattern work consistently, especially in diverse fisheries. Carrie Stevens herself, while she tied more for trout than salmon, is credited with originating over ninety patterns, many of which were for landlock fishing. And many other local and regional dressings have been conceived to fool the salmon in their respective waters.

One of the few things that serious landlock fly fishers generally agree on is that these creatures tend to be short strikers. This accounts for the popularity of long and extralong streamer hooks. Some anglers, notably those who like to troll the lakes, use tandem designs, with a dropper hook hanging to the rear. These are definitely effective, but they are no joy if you choose to cast instead of troll, especially in larger sizes. They also may be taken deep into the salmon's throat, sometimes together with the main hook. For these reasons, I stick to single hooks.

Traditional streamer hooks often employ the Limerick or improved-sproat bends. Though I have no great problem with using the so-called Model Perfect design, which is semicircular in shape, I do like the way in which the compound-curved bends look, and how they track in the water. Their shape also places the hook point a little farther to the rear.

Unlike fine-wire dry-fly hooks, streamer hooks work best if they have a fairly long, well-tapered point. This enables easier penetration with the heavier wire. However, a long-shanked hook shouldn't have too fine a wire, as that rare dream fish might be strong enough to bend it when heading for the open waters.

As to barbs, I like 'em small. It doesn't take a huge barb to hold even the most acrobatic of landlocks; in fact, too high a barb can inhibit effective engagement. And it goes without saying that a smaller barb enables easy release with negligible effect on the fish.

As to the front end of the hook, there are choices there as well. Eyes that are turned up or down are fine, so long as the angle is not extreme. Personally, I prefer a straight eye, because it works well with the loop-type knots I use when fishing this type of streamer. I also like what is called a looped eye, which features a return wire. This provides a better foundation for setting materials in place, and also eliminates any rough edges around the closure of the eye that might abrade a tippet.

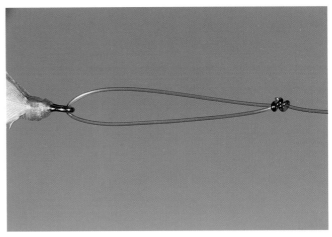

A straight-eyed hook works very well with the various loop knots that experienced streamer fishers prefer for the improvement of the fly's action in the water.

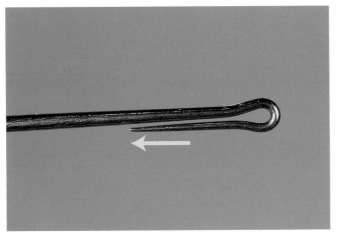

If you opt for a looped-eye hook, choose one with a well-tapered return wire, such as the Daiichi model 2370.

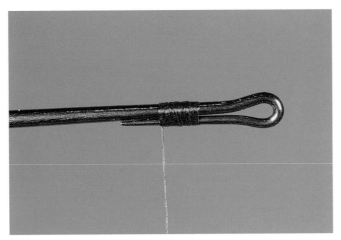

Tie on over the double wire, thus bringing it and the main shank together, eliminating any gap between the two.

Getting back to patterns: While landlocks are frequently caught on rather outlandish "attractor" flies, I personally prefer a dressing that bears some resemblance to a prevalent forage fish—in this case, the smelt. This is what I had in mind when I worked out the dressing for the Winnie Boy during the winter of 2002.

I'm married to a Russian lady, and she has some rather colorful expressions in her native language that refer to the fisherman that comes home empty-handed, suggesting that he may have been engaged in other pursuits. So once or twice a year, I bring home a nice, fat landlock for the table. Most of my landlocks are caught in Lake Winnepesaukee and around the mouths of its feeder streams. An examination of stomach contents often reveals a predominance of smelt—specifically, small ones. These are referred to as "pin smelt."

Landlocked salmon seem to prefer to take their food in small bites. This is true of even the good-size ones—and I've caught them up to 4 pounds in recent years. I've noticed that often the little smelt are swallowed tail-first. This may account for the salmon's preference for pin smelt, and also for their tendency to be short strikers.

THE WINNIE BOY STREAMER

On that note, the Winnie Boy. As it might imply, the Winnie Boy takes its name from Lake Winnepesaukee. However, feedback from friend anglers to whom I have given flies to try indicates that this fly will work on different species in different waters. My colleagues in the Catskills have caught some large trout with them in the Beaverkill and Delaware Rivers.

The creation of the Winnie Boy was inspired by a shipment of hen capes from Dr. Tom Whiting. These are the females of the large American Hackle strain, which also produces the roosters that Dr. Whiting raises for saltwater, salmon-fly, bass-fly, and streamer tying. They are available in both natural and dyed colors. The naturals come in various shades of dun or gray. The shape and texture of these feathers make them ideal for tying "wings" (I've never been comfortable with that term!) on imitative streamers.

Here's the basic dressing for the Winnie Boy:

Hook:	Long streamer; here, the Daiichi model 2370.
Thread:	Fine, medium gray; here, 8/0 Uni-Thread.
Body:	Any multicolored synthetic material, such as rainbow Flashabou, wrapped, and coated with some tough adhesive.
Belly:	White hair.
Wings:	Two natural or dyed dun gray American hen hackle cape feathers.
Cheeks:	Two natural or dyed dun gray American hen hackle saddle feathers.
Eyes:	Mylar stick-ons, fixed in place with a tiny drop of Zap-A-Gap.

On this pattern, small feathers from the hen saddle are also used. A little preparation is required:

1. Select two well-matched cape feathers, strip them to size, and put a small droplet of Zap-A-Gap or similar adhesive precisely at the little "delta" at the front.
2. Select two saddle feathers, stick the eyes on, then Zap-A-Gap them also.
3. Lay the feathers out to dry on a piece of waxed paper. Lay them curved-sides-down, so they don't stick to the paper. Don't use them until they are completely dry.

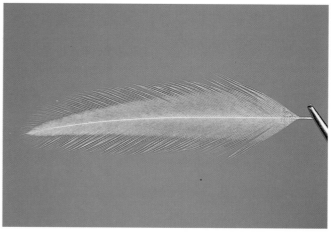

1. This is an ideal feather for this pattern, well shaped, with some web in the center. You'll need a matched pair.

2. Place a tiny drop of Zap-A-Gap here at the juncture of the hackle and quill on each of the two feathers. This will ensure that the feathers stay put when tied in place.

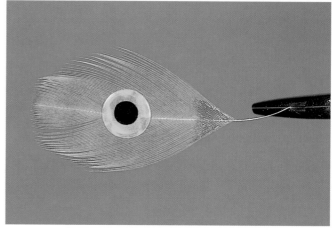

3. Select a pair of hen saddle feathers for the cheeks, and press the eyes into place. Then Zap-A-Gap at the juncture, as you did with the main feathers in step 2.

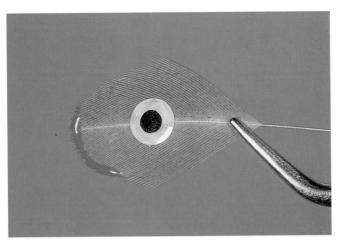

4. As an option, a gill effect can be created by tinting the edge of the cheek feather with red water-base acrylic paint.

A most useful adhesive for protecting fly bodies made of floss, tinsel, or just about any vulnerable body wrap is Soft Body, from Angler's Choice, which is a brand name used by a company called Gone Fishin' Enterprises. The web address is a lengthy one: www.anglerschoiceflytyingmaterials.com.

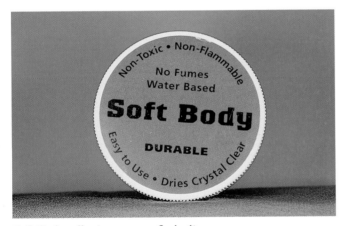

Soft Body adhesive protects fly bodies.

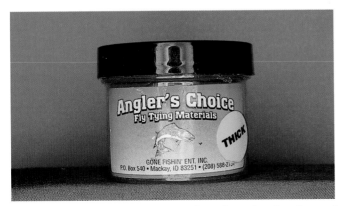

If it gets too thick, you can thin Soft Body with a few drops of water or rubbing alcohol.

This is a water-base product, which I really like. Not only is it free from noxious fumes, but it's also very easy to thin, should it get too thick. You have two choices: a few drops of either water or rubbing alcohol. In either case, be very conservative; add just a drop or two at a time, and shake vigorously. Two viscosities are offered, appropriately named thick and thin.

An important note: All adhesives used in the preparatory steps must be completely dry before the fly is tied. You'll want to make up a supply of assemblies ahead of time, apply whatever adhesive, and lay them out on a sheet of waxed paper.

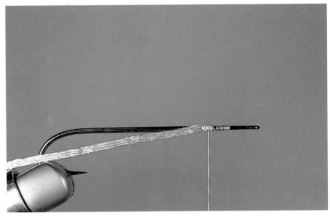

1. Tie in the body material at the front, but well back from the eye of the hook.

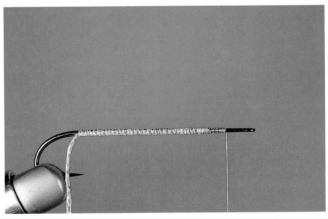

2. Reposition the body material by wrapping the thread over it to the bend, then forward to the tie-in position. Burying the body material helps form a smooth base.

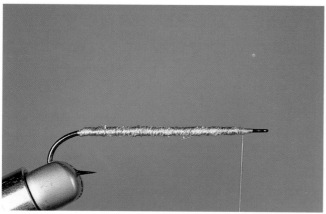

3. Wrap the body material, overlapping the turns slightly to make it go on smoothly, then tie it off and trim the excess.

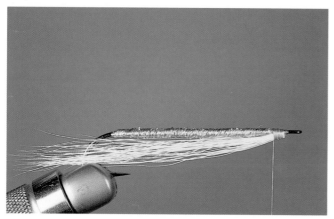

4. The belly hair is tied in at the "throat" and should extend slightly beyond the rear of the hook.

5. Be sure the Zap-A-Gap has dried completely. Then tie on the wing feathers along the sides of the hook, passing the thread over the very front where the Zap-A-Gap was applied. Secure them, and trim off the quills.

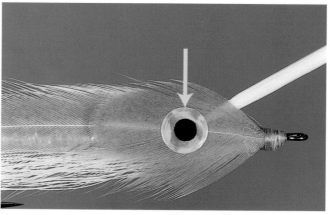

6. Do the same with the cheek feathers, again making sure the Zap-A-Gap has dried completely. Tie off the thread with a whip finish. Then hold each cheek feather out from the wings, and apply a tiny droplet of Zap-A-Gap only to the back side of the eye. Now allow the cheeks to fall back in place.

7. The finished fly.

This is a really simple fly to tie. Just follow the photo sequence and captions. Notice that the "wing" feathers shroud the body, rather than ride above it. When the fly is wet, the coloration of the body material glows through the translucent wings in a subtle, enticing manner.

Take note that I use only two feathers for the wings. Most streamer dressings call for four or six. However, the unique semiopaqueness of these feathers allows two to suffice.

The Winnie Boy can be fished either trolling or casting. And if you want to alter the colors, go right ahead. I have noticed that landlocked smelt vary in shading from one lake to another.

UNCLE DICKIE'S DACE

If you want, you can also imitate different forage fish. For example, here's a Black-Nosed Dace pattern that I've named Uncle Dickie's Dace:

Hook:	Long streamer; here, the Daiichi model 2370.
Thread:	Black 8/0 Uni-Thread or similar.
Tag (optional):	Red or orange Uni-Stretch.
Body:	Flat silver tinsel.
Belly:	White hair.
Wings:	Four furnace hackle feathers: brown or ginger, with a dark stripe down the center.
Cheeks:	None.
Eyes:	Mylar stick-ons, fixed in place with a tiny drop of Zap-A-Gap.

1. Select feathers to form two pairs: a front and a back. Stick an eye on the outside feather of each pair in the position shown.

2. "Spoon" the feathers together into pairs. Place a tiny droplet of Zap-A-Gap at the very front, as was done on the Winnie Boy, and also onto the back side of the eyes. Allow the assemblies to dry completely.

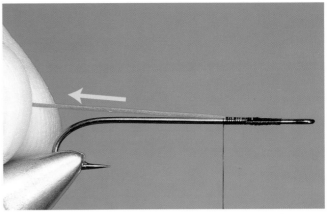

3. Tie on in the position shown, then tie in the Uni-Stretch for the butt.

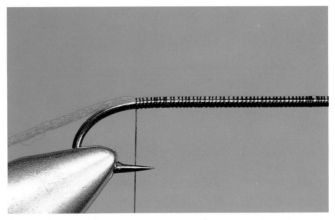

4. While pulling from the rear, wrap the thread neatly over the Uni-Stretch, almost to the bend. This method makes it easy to control the Uni-Stretch while binding it down to form a smooth underbody.

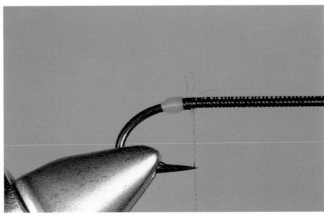

5. Wrap the Uni-Stretch to form the butt, then trim off the excess.

6. Tie in the body material at the rear, adjacent to the butt.

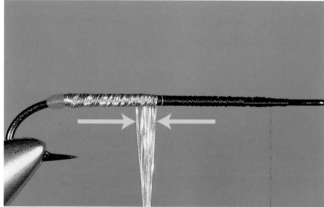

7. To form a smooth, flat body, allow the material to spread a little as you wrap.

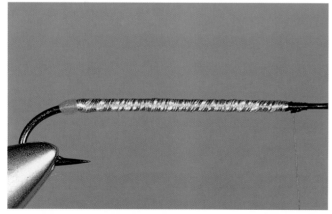

8. Complete the body and trim off the excess material, leaving some space up front.

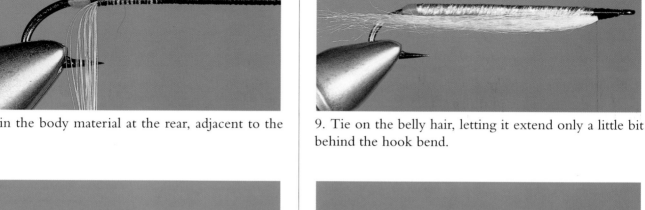

9. Tie on the belly hair, letting it extend only a little bit behind the hook bend.

10. Tie on the hackle fiber throat, and in the process, wrap a smooth base on which to set the main feathers.

11. Tie on the two pairs of feathers, as was done on the Winnie Boy. A whip finish then completes the Uncle Dickie's Dace.

Okay, why have I used four feathers here, when I used only two on the Winnie Boy? It's because they are from a rooster cape, rather than a hen cape, and they lack the denseness and web of the hen feathers.

A Novel Streamer Design

IN THIS CHAPTER YOU'LL LEARN
1. How to use a mallard flank feather for the body of a fly.
2. A different method for tying on Krystal Flash.
3. The incorporation of bead and cone heads.

In the winter of 1979, I taught my first weekend tying class for Hunter's Angling Supplies. At that time, the store was located in the house of the original proprietor, Bill Hunter, in New Boston, New Hampshire. The class took place in the attic.

I had ten students. One of them was a gentleman from nearby Manchester named Nick Lambrou. He was, and is, a local legend as an angler and tier. My most vivid remembrance of Nick from that weekend was that when I announced that our next fly would be the infamous Hornberg, he excused himself and left the room. I was informed that Nick considered the Hornberg as being tantamount to baitfishing and was offended that I would include it in the agenda.

Subsequently, I was to learn that this was a practical joke, meant to shake me up a little, which it did. As it turned out, Nick had actually evolved the Hornberg into a much more effective fly. He called it the Heron.

The distinguishing characteristic of the Heron is the unique manner in which a flank feather from a mallard is used. Instead of simply being tied on, it is wrapped as a "collar," so to speak. The technique is virtually the same as tying a collar hackle on a salmon fly. However, the mallard feather forms the body of the fly, not the hackle.

This great brook trout took my orange-collared Heron at Awesome Lake, Labrador. That's Mr. Wally Harris, guide and friend, holding it.

Dick Soares with a nice Winnepesaukee landlock that took the Heron fly.

Dick with an incredible brook trout, also caught on the Heron.

THE MALLARD HERON

There are now quite a few versions of the Heron, and I really can't say which one was Nick's original dressing; maybe none of them. Here's one I use a lot, and with excellent results:

Hook: Long nymph or short streamer; here, the Daiichi model 1750, 4XL.
Thread: Fine, medium gray; here, 8/0 Uni-Thread.
Underbody: Flat silver tinsel.
Main body: One or two barred mallard flank feathers.
Hackle: A soft gray hen cape or saddle feather.

The trick here is to wrap the flank feather in such a manner that it envelops the hook as an elongated cornucopia. You'll see how this is done in the tying sequence.

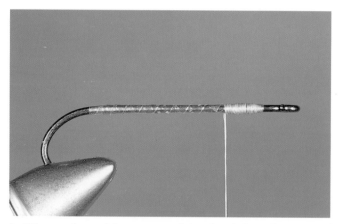

1. Tie on about 30 percent of the shank length rearward of the eye, and tie in the body material. Then wrap the material to the bend and back to the tie-in spot, forming a two-layer body. Tie off and trim the material, leaving lots of space up front—at least a quarter of the hook shank.

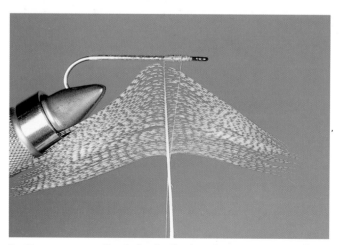

2. Prepare a mallard flank feather by stripping off the fuzzy material around the butt end. Stroke the barbs so

that they stand out straight from the quill, then tie the feather in by the tip end, with the cupped side facing inward, as shown here.

3. While holding the feather by the butt end of the quill, under sufficient tension to keep the quill straight, carefully stroke back the fibers so that they all lie to the rear of the quill. Don't allow any of them to cross over; they should stay on their own respective sides.

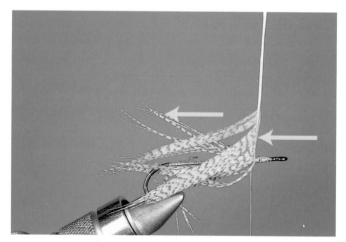

4. Wrap the feather as you would an elongated collar hackle. The quill is the leading edge. As you wrap the feather, keep on stroking back the fibers, and try to make them stay cupped-sides-inward. If they should get hung up around the hook point or vise head, help them along with your fingers. The idea is to form a cornucopia.

5. This is how the mallard feather should appear after it's been wrapped. If a few of the fibers appear to stick out awkwardly, don't worry; they will fall into place as soon as you cast the fly into the water.

6. Prepare a small hen hackle feather in the same manner as you did the mallard feather, and tie it in by the tip end, dull-side-inward.

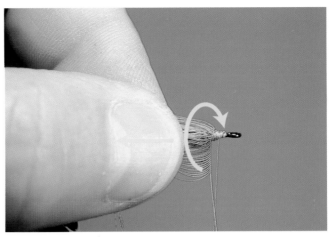

7. Make a collar hackle by stroking back the fibers as you wrap.

8. The completed fly, dry. If the fibers seem to cling together, pass a fine-tooth comb through them a few times.

9. The completed fly, wet.

Adding a bead or cone head can enhance the potency of this fly. Here's a beadhead pattern:

Hook:	Same as before.
Thread:	8/0 Uni-Thread or similar.
Bead:	Here, a black fly-tying bead, size $1/8$ inch.
Flash:	Two strands of pearl Krystal Flash, doubled back.
Body:	None.
Main feather:	Barred mallard, same as before.
Front feather:	Gray mottled hen cape or saddle; here, a Brahma hen saddle feather.

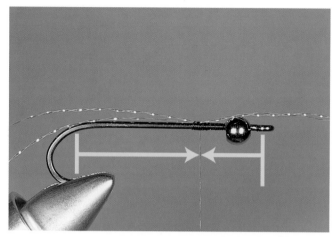

1. Debarb the hook and run the bead all the way to the front. Be sure to insert the point of the hook into the smaller side of the hole drilled through the bead, so that the larger aperture faces rearward. Then wrap down the hook about one-third of the way back from the eye, and tie in the two strands of Krystal Flash by the center.

2. Double back the Krystal Flash and wrap over the doubled spot, so that you have a total of four strands extending rearward.

3. Just forward of the Krystal Flash, tie in the prepared mallard feather by the tip end, cupped-side-inward, and wrap it according to the instructions for the previous fly.

4. Prepare and tie in the feather that will form the collar, also according to the instructions for the previous fly.

5. Form the collar, wrapping the feather up close to the bead. Then wrap just enough thread to allow the bead to slide back into place and envelop those wraps, but to go no farther.

6. Tie off, then tie back on in front of the bead. Wrap enough thread to force the bead into position, and secure it. Whip-finish again, and the fly is done.

And here's yet another variation of the Heron. It features a cone head and uses brown mallard as the main feather and hot orange for the collar. It's a great brook trout pattern and is also effective on landlocked salmon. The dressing:

Hook:	Same as before.
Thread:	8/0 Uni-Thread or similar.
Bead:	Here, a gold cone head, size $1/8$ inch.
Flash:	Two strands of pearl Krystal Flash, doubled back.
Body:	None.
Main feather:	Brown mallard.
Front feather:	Hen cape or saddle feather, dyed hot orange.

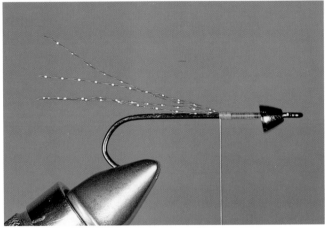

1. Debarb the hook, slide the cone into place, and apply the Krystal Flash as per the instructions for the beadhead pattern.

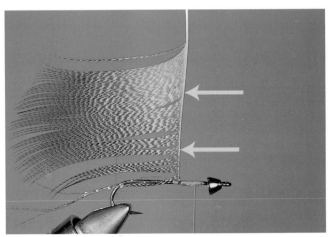

2. Strip off the material from the short side of a brown mallard feather, leaving the longer, nicely marked fibers on the other side. Tie it in by the tip.

3. Wrap the brown mallard feather the same as you would a whole feather, as shown in the previous examples.

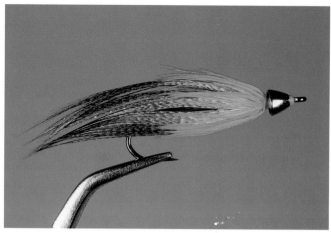

5. The completed fly.

4. Wrap the collar, also as shown in the previous examples.

The Joys of Uni-Stretch

12

IN THIS CHAPTER YOU'LL LEARN
1. The multiple uses of Uni-Stretch.
2. Tying with Thin Skin.

I have always loved stoneflies. I first became acquainted with them in my fledgling days as an aspiring fly fisher on the Esopus Creek in New York's Catskills. As I learned about the aquatic bugs that fed the trout and helped the angler, I began to notice the empty casings of stonefly nymphs on the streamside rocks. Rolling a stone or two revealed these fascinating creatures. I was amazed by their beauty. The yellow-bellied Perlidae looked like intricate mosaics, and the dark, almost black Pteronarcyidae seemed as fierce as little dragons.

It was love at first sight, and I would eventually discover that I had lots of company. The inimitable Paul Schmookler, master fly dresser, responded to a question about party affiliation during a political telephone interview as follows: "I'm a Plecopteran!"

Back then, the Esopus was a good stonefly stream, and a simple Montana nymph was usually all one needed to deceive the gullible rainbows that abounded there, and sometimes a brown or two as well. As I ventured farther afield, however, I found that more realistic imitations often produced better results. After all, these insects get pretty big, and the fish get a good look at them.

Stonefly nymphs have exoskeletons and must shed their skins in order to grow. This transition is known as an instar period. Since these creatures have long subaquatic lives, some as long as four years, they are present in a variety of sizes in the stream. They are most active just prior to emergence, but they are always there and available to the trout. Thus, using imitations in a variety of sizes often bears fruit.

I've written about stonefly nymphs before, in books and magazines. The evolution of new materials has inspired me to revisit them. The pattern shown here is the most recent step in this evolution. Its appeal is that it combines realism with simplicity of tying. It's versatile;

you can use various colors to imitate whichever stonefly nymphs you want. I have had a lot of success fishing a black stonefly nymph. Here, however, I'm going to tie it in brown, because it shows photographic detail much better.

Stonefly nymphs work great in the Gunnison River, even in December.

57

I'll introduce you to two enabling materials: Uni-Stretch, a spooled cross between thread and floss that is available in many colors, and Thin Skin, a product of Wapsi Fly, Inc. The joy of Uni-Stretch is that it works great in a bobbin and goes on like spray paint. A perfectly smooth-tipped bobbin tube is a necessity. If yours is the least bit flawed, you'll find out immediately, as the Uni-Stretch becomes a fuzzball. My favorite is the Griffin Supreme, which features a ceramic "donut" at the business end of the tube.

Thin Skin is available in a number of colors and in several patterned variations that make great golden stonefly nymphs. You simply cut it into strips with a straightedge and a razor blade or craft knife, peel it from the paper backing, and tie it in place. One word of caution: Keep it out of contact with any adhesives used in the construction of the fly, including head lacquer, as the thinners will eat away at the colored coating of the Thin Skin.

As to hooks, there are a number of them that will work, so the choice is yours. A long-shanked nymph hook, such as the Daiichi model 1750, works okay. However, for appearance' sake, I prefer a hook with a graceful curvature, such as the Daiichi model 1270 or 1870.

SIMPLE STONEFLY NYMPH

Here's the dressing for the Simple Stonefly Nymph. The components are listed in the order in which they are tied in, this being an important aspect of the tying process.

Hook:	As suggested; here, a Daiichi 1270.
Thread:	Brown Uni-Stretch, also regular brown tying thread, 6/0 or 8/0.
Foundation:	Strips of fairly thick lead-free wire or, if you prefer, heavy monofilament.
Shell and wing cases:	Brown Thin Skin.
Tails:	Two brown biots.
Ribbing:	Fine monofilament; here, dark Maxima leader material.
Hackle:	Soft-textured brown rooster or hen.
Thorax:	Brown dubbing or yarn; here, dark brown Uni-Yarn.
Wing case dividers:	The Maxima.
Adhesive:	Zap-A-Gap or equivalent.

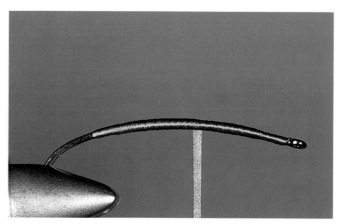

1. Mount the Uni-Stretch in a bobbin, tie on near the front, and wrap several layers, forming a smooth base. Note: As the Uni-Stretch becomes twisted due to the wrapping action, give the bobbin a few spins counterclockwise (clockwise for lefties) to flatten it.

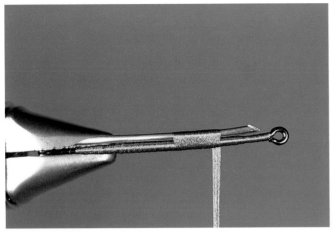

2. Prepare a wire strip by cutting it to length and taper-cutting both ends, then tie it along the side of the hook. It should reach just to the bend at the rear and just short of the hook eye up front.

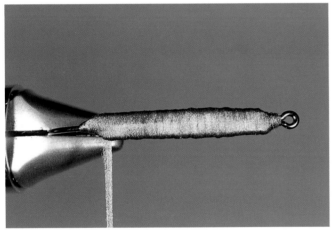

3. Prepare another wire strip that's a mirror image of the first, tie it in on the opposite side, and cover both strips with a couple layers of Uni-Stretch. This shapes the nymph body and adds a little weight.

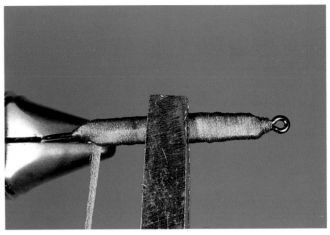

4. Squeeze the assembly with flat-jawed pliers to ensure that the strips lie flat along each side of the hook.

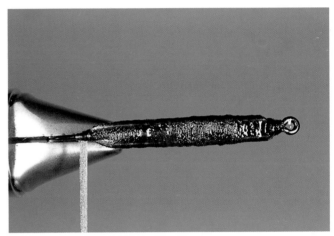

5. Saturate the assembly with Zap-A-Gap or comparable superglue, and rub it with a toothpick or Q-Tip until it's completely dry.

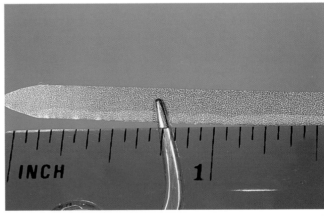

6. Cut a strip of Thin Skin to shape, tapering one end.

7. Separate the Thin Skin from the backing.

8. Tie in the Thin Skin by the tapered end and let it lie to the rear, off the back of the hook.

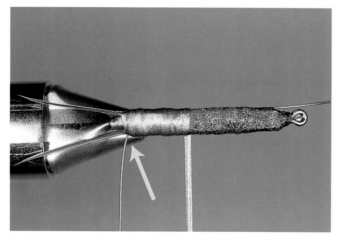

9. Tie a biot on each side of the hook at the rear, just ahead of where the Thin Skin is hanging, then tie in a piece of monofilament for the ribbing.

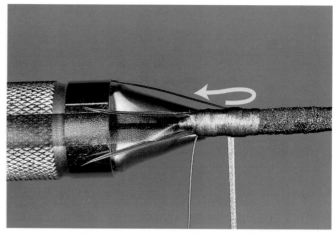

10. Double back the butt end of the monofilament, bind it down, and trim off the excess, thus ensuring that the ribbing material will not pull out.

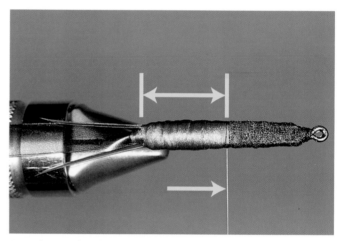

11. Shape the body, finishing with the Uni-Stretch at about the halfway point. Tie off the Uni-Stretch, and tie on with the regular thread.

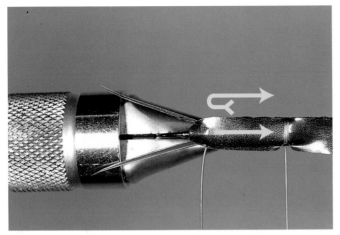

12. Fold the Thin Skin forward and tie it down.

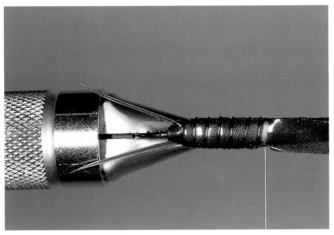

13. Spiral-wrap the ribbing. This forms the segments and shapes the body.

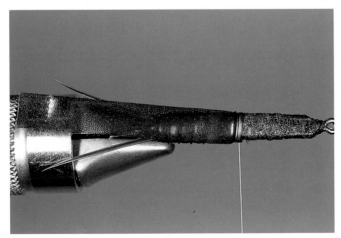

14. Fold back the remaining Thin Skin, and tie it down with a few thread wraps. Let it lie to the rear as before.

15. Fold the hackle feather by stroking back all fibers on both sides of the quill, and tie it in by the tip end at the front of the body.

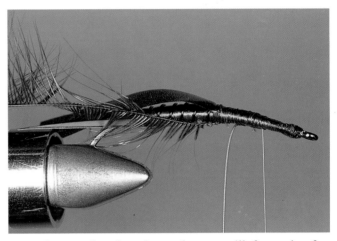

16. Advance the thread to where you'll form the first wing case—about one-third of the distance from the front end of the body to the eye—and tie in another piece of the monofilament, doubling back the butt end as before, to prevent slipping. Let it hang down for the moment.

17. Wrap back to the front of the body, and tie in a piece of Uni-Yarn.

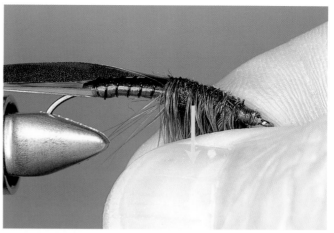

19. Wrap the hackle, stroke the barbs downward, and cut off the ones that remain on top.

18. Wrap the Uni-Yarn back and forth, working around the hanging monofilament, to form the thorax, then tie it off near the front.

20. Fold the Thin Skin forward, bind it down, double it back, and wrap over it to secure it Cut off the excess.

21. Form the first wing case by working the monofilament through the hackle.

22. Form the second wing case by working the monofilament through the hackle again, then tie it off. This also forms the front segment, which is called the pronotum. Whip-finish, and the fly is done.

23. Top view.

At first glance, this nymph may seem complicated, but if you follow the photo sequence in order, it's surprisingly easy. Incidentally, the thorax material represents the gills of the nymph. Tease it out a bit, so it's fuzzy and can collect air bubbles.

For those of you who like to chase the formidable steelhead of New York's Salmon River and other Great Lakes feeders, tie this nymph in black, except for the thorax, which employs some brilliant color, such as hot pink, ice blue, or chartreuse. I suggest tying it smaller: sizes 10 to 14. For some reason, the steelies seem to prefer small flies.

13

More Joys Of Uni-Stretch

IN THIS CHAPTER YOU'LL LEARN
1. The use of Uni-Stretch for Spey flies.
2. Substituting with synthetic dubbing for Spey flies.
3. How to make ring-necked pheasant Spey hackles.
4. Substituting rooster Spey hackle for heron.

One of the most popular flies in the glory years of Scottish salmon fishing was the so-called Spey fly, named after the River Spey. The elongated hackle was tied with feathers from either the great blue or the smaller black heron. If one were to use these materials today, he or she would be in considerably more jeopardy than the fish, as they are strictly protected.

A modest-size steelhead from the Cheektowaga that took a Spey fly.

To digress from fly tying for a moment, while I certainly agree in principal with the protection of threatened wildlife, this concept is brought into question when one protected species proliferates to the endangerment of others. Here in the United States, such is the case with the great blue heron. They have no natural enemies of significance, and they are lethal predators. From what I've personally observed, they kill everything they can get their beaks into, and I've seen many skewered fish along the shores of lakes and ponds that were not eaten by their assassins.

An acquaintance of mine runs a commercial fish hatchery, and he has to cover all of the rearing ponds with chicken wire, or he'd be out of business in a day or two. If I understand correctly, persons who operate such facilities can get permits from the federal government to kill blue herons. However, the carcasses must be destroyed, feathers and all.

What a waste! Wouldn't it be reasonable to allow these fantastic feathers to be sold to fly tiers? Wouldn't that be a win-win situation? But it seems that once politics gets into the act, all common sense and logic go out the window.

In recent years, Spey flies have become popular again, as they are effective in fishing for steelhead trout, both in their natural habitat in the Pacific Northwest and in the estuaries of the Great Lakes, where they were transplanted years ago. This has created a demand for heron feather substitutes. Smaller Spey flies and so-called pseudo-Speys can be tied with rump feathers from a cock ring-necked pheasant. This limits size, however, as these feathers are only a fraction the size of heron feathers.

Enter Dr. Tom Whiting, aka Chicken Superman. Tom is developing a strain of chickens that will yield Spey hackle. At this writing (summer of 2003), the birds are only into their third generation, but they are already showing amazing progress, and by the time this book is in print, pelts should be available in quantity. Tom has been kind enough to send me some of these feathers, so let's put them to use.

UNCLE DICKIE'S STEELY SPEY

Here's a typical Spey fly that works for both salmon and steelhead. It further underscores what a versatile material Uni-Stretch is. I call it Uncle Dickie's Steely Spey. Here's the dressing:

Hook:	Typical Spey; here, the Daiichi Alec Jackson, model 2050.
Thread:	First fuschia Uni-Stretch, then regular black thread.
Ribbing:	Heavy gold oval tinsel.
Rear body:	The Uni-Stretch.
Hackle:	One or two gray-dyed Whiting Farms rooster Spey hackles.
Front body:	Glitzy synthetic dubbing; here, purple Ice Dub.
Wings:	Two strips of white goose shoulder feather, aka goose body.

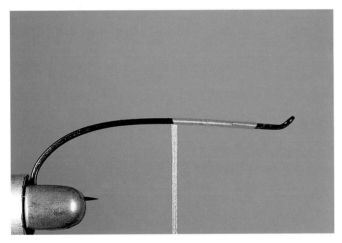

1. With the Uni-Stretch, tie on over the double wire near the eye of the hook, and wrap smoothly to the center of the hook.

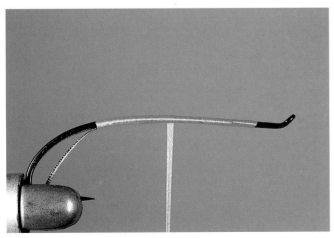

2. Tie in the ribbing tinsel at this spot and smoothly bind it down, wrapping over it to a position directly above the hook point. Then wrap back to the center.

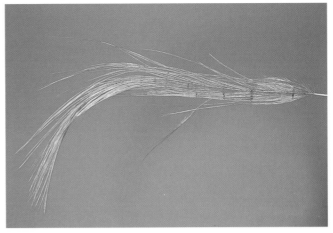

3. A typical Whiting Farms rooster Spey hackle.

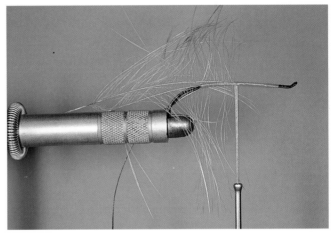

4. Tie in the feather by the tip end at about the center of the hook. For a more dense hackle, tie in two feathers at once, as I have done here.

5. Stroke the feather back out of the way, spin on some dubbing material, and begin wrapping the front part of the body.

6. Finish the dubbing, leaving adequate space at the front for the wing, and switch to regular black thread.

7. Stroke the hackle feather forward, gathering all of the fibers, and make one or two thread wraps over it at the eye. This is done simply to keep it out of the way during the first few turns of the ribbing process.

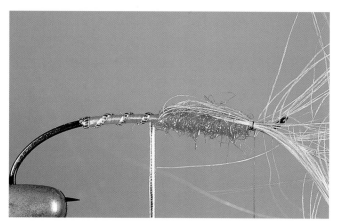

8. Begin wrapping the ribbing by taking an extra turn at the rear to form a small tag, then take several well-spaced turns forward, stopping when you reach the tie-in location of the hackle feather.

9. Release the hackle feather, fold it back out of the way, and finish wrapping the ribbing by taking four or five spaced turns over the dubbing. Don't crowd the eye.

10. Wrap the hackle, abutting the rear edges of the tinsel turns, stroking back the barbs as you go. Take an extra turn or two at the front of the body to fill out that area, secure the feather, and trim off all excess material.

11. Stroke the barbs downward a few times, inducing them to go to whichever side of the hook they naturally want to go to.

12. With tweezers, pluck out any barbs that refuse to be stroked downward. Resist the temptation to simply cut them off, as this leaves stubble.

13. Here's what the finished hackle should look like.

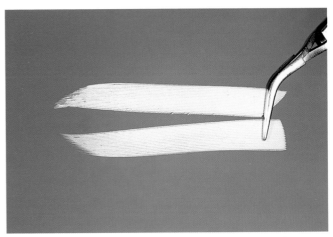

14. Cut two narrow strips from opposite sides of a goose body feather.

15. Spoon the strips, laying them one atop the other, curved-sides-down. Stroke them toward the tips until they are as straight as they are willing to get and appear as a single strip. Then center them over the hook, curved-sides-down, shroud them just a bit around the "shoulders" of the fly, and tie them on, beginning with soft, gathering wraps. Reposition as necessary to get the wing strips to lie straight down the center of the hook shank.

16. Finish the fly by securing the wing, trimming the butts, wrapping a neat head, and doing a whip finish.

I should also mention that the new synthetic dubbings, of which there are many, are excellent substitutes for seal fur, another material that in the past was widely used in fly tying. In fact, I think they are better than real seal's fur. The fish might feel quite differently about that, as seals are very effective predators. Migratory fish are terrified of them and, if they had a consciousness, would certainly wish them all dead. But they don't get to vote.

Some of these dubbings are easier to work with than others. Ice Dub, the one I'm using here, is remarkably user-friendly for a glossy, shiny material. It can be spun onto either thread or Uni-Stretch readily, without resorting to a dubbing loop or sticky wax. I'm sure there are others that are similar, but I also know firsthand that certain dubbings of this type are like trying to dub toothbrush bristles. See if you can try out dubbings before you end up buying stuff that will bring out the worst in your disposition down the road.

MALLARD FLANK SPEY

A workable, if not beautiful, Spey fly can be hackled with mallard flank. This is dense material, so only use half a feather; strip off the fibers from one side. After completing the fly, pass a fine-tooth comb through the hackle to separate the fibers.

Hook:	Typical Spey; here, the Daiichi Alec Jackson, model 2050.
Thread:	First chartreuse Uni-Stretch, then regular black thread.
Ribbing:	Heavy silver oval tinsel.
Rear body:	The Uni-Stretch.
Hackle:	One side of a mallard flank feather.
Front body:	Glitzy chartreuse synthetic dubbing.
Wings:	Two strips of gray goose tertial wing feather; the softer ones well back into the wing.

1. Follow the same procedure as with the previous fly, tying in the half-stripped mallard feather as shown.

2. Finish the fly, following the instructions for the previous fly.

RING-NECKED PHEASANT PSEUDO-SPEY

Though rump feathers from a cock ring-necked pheasant also make fine Spey hackles, they don't get very big, so size is limited. I guess you'd have to classify such flies as pseudo-Speys. Pseudo or whatever, they fish very well. Here's a dressing I like:

Hook:	Typical Spey; here, the Daiichi Alec Jackson, model 2050.
Thread:	First Silver Doctor Blue Uni-Stretch, then regular black thread.
Ribbing:	Medium silver oval tinsel; three turns over the front body.
Rear body:	Flat tinsel, silver or pearlescent.
Hackle:	The largest cock ring-necked pheasant rump feather you can lay your hands on.
Front body:	The Uni-Stretch.
Wings:	Same as the mallard chartreuse pattern; two strips of gray goose tertial wing feather.

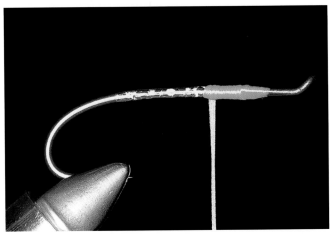

1. Tie on and wrap the rear portion of the body, covering about the rear 60 percent of the hook.

2. Prepare the pheasant feather, stripping off the fluff at the butt end. Tie it in by the tip, then tie in the ribbing tinsel. Build up the front body a little with the Uni-

Stretch, tie it off, and switch to black thread. Then wrap the three turns of ribbing, tie off the tinsel, and trim the excess.

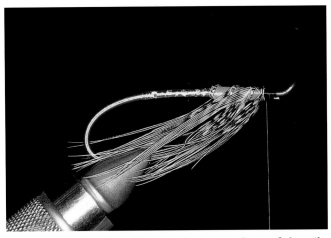

3. Wrap the hackle, abutting the rear edges of the ribbing tinsel. Tie it off and trim. Configure it with the stroking-and-pruning process, and wrap a smooth base for the wing.

4. Add the wing just as was done on the previous Spey flies. This completes the fly.

The Spey hook you see here is a variation of the traditional Atlantic salmon hook. It features a looped, turned-up eye. This sort of eye accommodates an "around-the-neck" type of knot. In the bygone days of organic gut leaders, anglers used a Turle knot. Today our wonderfully strong synthetic leaders require a more secure knot, as they tend to be a bit slippery. Here you see the specialist loop knot, which has never failed me, except when I screwed up the tying.

In the illustrations, you see the front end of a typical Atlantic salmon fly. Note that a bit of bare hook shows in front of the head. This helps in seating the loop part of the knot around the neck of the fly, with the leader extending straight out through the eye.

2. The knot is formed and the loop is passed over the fly, as with a Turle knot.

1. Notice that space has been left for the knot.

3. The knot, tightened. Notice how the leader extends straight through the eye.

A Simple and Simply Great Foam Innovation

14

IN THIS CHAPTER YOU'LL LEARN

1. Tying with foam.
2. Making a dubbed body and ribbing it in one operation.

A lady guide of my acquaintance lives in north-central Massachusetts. She specializes in guiding on nearby rivers in her home state and in Connecticut, and she knows them extremely well. Anyone who wants to learn how to catch trout on these tough waters, and isn't frightened by the prospect of being outfished by a woman, would do well to spend a day with Marla Blair. Her website address is www.marlablair.com.

Left: *Marla Blair doing her thing with the Jailbird.* Above: *The author with a Jailbird-eating brown trout.*

THE JAILBIRD

One of Marla's go-to flies is called the Jailbird. It's a very simple little pattern—so much so that in the beginning, I discounted it. A day onstream with Marla made a believer out of me; the Jailbird fooled the cerebral trout of the Farmington River, who have seen it all and want no part of most of it. Marla says she ties this fly in sizes 16 to 20.

Simple as the Jailbird is to tie, you need to follow a specific sequence of steps. Here's one of the dressings I like:

Hook:	A shrimp/scud model, such as the Daiichi model 1130.
Thread:	Red 6/0 Uni-Thread for size 14–16, 8/0 for size 18–20.
Wing case: (for lack of a better term)	A narrow strip of white foam.
Body/thorax:	Your choice of dubbing; Marla uses Universal Vise, Ultra-Fine, Blue-Winged Olive.
Ribbing:	The tying thread.

There are any number of foams that will work for this fly. The one I like the best is a product of the Larva Lace Company. It's labeled White Dry Fly foam and comes precut into strips, some of which are ⅛ inch wide and some ¼. Larva Lace offers some very useful products. The web address is www.larvalace.com.

This foam is very easy to work with, being softer than most other closed-cell foams. The precut strips can be reduced in width simply by pulling on them, which slims the strip down. This allows you to adapt the strip to the size of the fly you are tying.

Perhaps the most critical factor in tying the Jailbird is to use just enough dubbing so that you run out just as you reach the rear end of the body. This is what shapes the fly. By wrapping the dubbing rearward, then wrapping the thread forward, the ribbing crosses over the dubbing in the reverse direction, so it doesn't sink into the dubbing and get lost.

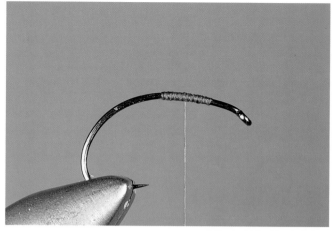

1. Tie on and wrap a thread base where the foam strip will be tied in.

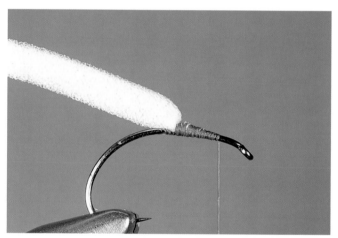

2. Tie in the strip by the tip, with the long part extending rearward.

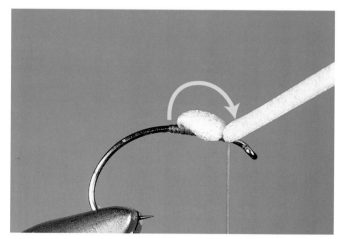

3. Bury the butt end with thread, then fold the strip forward and tie it down, thus creating a ball of foam.

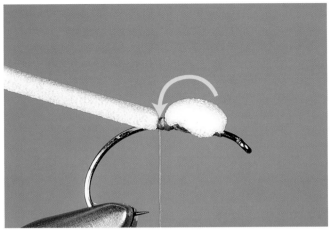

4. Move the thread to the rear of the ball. Bring the strip back over, thus forming a two-layer ball, and tie it down.

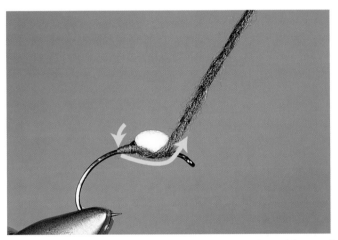

5. Trim off the excess foam, and with the thread located just to the rear of the wing case, spin on a narrow worm of soft dubbing and wrap it forward, passing under the foam ball.

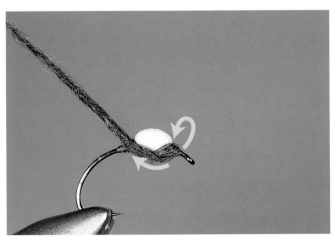

6. Take one or two front-back crisscross wraps, forming a "thorax" beneath the wing case.

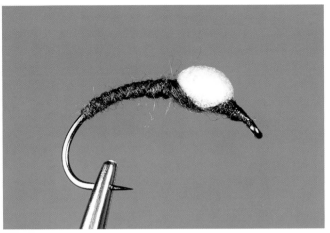

7. Wrap the dubbing to the rear of the hook and down around the bend a little. Then finish the fly by spiral-wrapping the thread forward, passing it under the foam ball, and tying off at the eye.

The Jailbird is tied small and smaller. I have suggested to Marla that under a 16, it might be called the Jailbait. However, since hook sizes get smaller as the number gets higher, there's a contradiction there. Too bad.

This fly fishes most effectively as a dropper suspended from a strike indicator, which could be of the foam or yarn type, or a large, buoyant dry fly, such as a Wulff pattern. Believe me, it works. A friend of mine caught a 22-inch rainbow on it in the Madison River, and a steelhead in the New York Salmon River running into Lake Ontario. That's proof enough for me.

15

Huge Dry Flies

IN THIS CHAPTER YOU'LL LEARN
1. A method of tying the Hewitt Skater.
2. A different quill-type body.
3. A method for keeping large-hackled flies from twisting the leader.

Edward Ringwood Hewitt was one of the legendary figures of the early to mid-1900s—the so-called golden era of northeastern fly fishing. Apparently he was a very wealthy man, and he owned a sizable stretch of water on the Neversink River in the southern Catskills. Unfortunately, most of his water lies buried under the Neversink Reservoir, another sad testament to the greedy and irresponsible lust for water by New York City.

Hewitt authored several books, including *Telling on the Trout* (1926), *Handbook of Fly Fishing* (1933), *Nymph Fly Fishing* (1934), and *A Trout and Salmon Fisherman for Seventy-five Years* (1948). There was also *Secrets of the Salmon*; I do not have a publication date for that one. He was an important figure in the annals of American fly fishing, but not the most informative of individuals, and much of the material in his writings was anecdotal.

One of Hewitt's legacies is a unique dry fly known as the Skater. It consisted of just two huge hackles; talk about simplicity! Charles K. Fox, that affable gentleman dubbed the Chaucer of the Letort by Arnold Gingrich, was intrigued by the Skater and, after corresponding with Hewitt, was sent a small supply. Charley learned to make the flies dance across the water's surface, in accordance with Hewitt's design, and he reported in his writings that they produced on the intimidating limestone streams of Pennsylvania.

I have never seen a set of tying instructions for the Skater. Maybe it exists somewhere, but if so, I'm not aware of it. I can't remember where I read it, but I vaguely recall something about someone taking a Hewitt fly apart in order to find out how it was tied. Years ago, I tied some, using my own methodology. They were only partially successful. Eventually I would learn that there was a trick to tying the two hackles; they were wrapped cupped-side-against-cupped-side and met in the middle. Think about that for a moment; how does one tie off the damn thing?

I have come up with my own method for tying the Skater. I have no idea whether it's the same way Hewitt tied it, but it does work, and as a bonus, it has solved a problem with another type of large-hackled dry fly, the Variant.

The key to my method is wrapping one hackle in the conventional manner, meaning over and away from the tier, and the other in reverse, meaning under and toward the tier. This not only configures the hackle properly, but also—and this is very important—helps keep the fly from twisting the leader into a Slinky in a few casts.

THE HEWITT SKATER

Before stepping through the tying process, I should mention that the most frustrating problem is finding large hackles of adequate quality. This was not an issue in Hewitt's day—in fact, finding hackle smaller than a size 12 was the problem then. I have some old capes that I've hung on to, mainly for comparative reasons, and that's what I'll be using here.

So what does today's tier do? My best advice would be to go to the many fly-fishing shows around the country. There you will see feathers from various growers on display, and also some imported pelts. These may yield some Skater hackle. I'm also told that my friend Dr. Whiting is considering developing a strain of large-hackle roosters. If that should eventuate, God bless the man.

Two other suggestions: Use very fine tying thread and a short-shank dry-fly hook. You'll see why as we go through the tying steps. Here's the dressing, such as it is:

Hook: Short-shank dry fly, such as the Daiichi model 1640.
Thread: Anything fine; here, 8/0 Uni-Thread.
Hackle: Two large feathers, opposing one another.

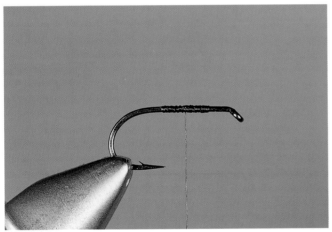

1. Tie on and wrap a thread base in the middle of the hook.

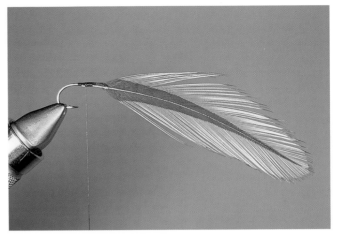

2. Tie in the first hackle feather in this position, dull side facing you, leaving just a bit of bare quill exposed.

3. Tie in the second hackle feather in this position, again dull side facing you, leaving just a bit of bare quill exposed. Leave the tying thread at that location.

4. Wrap the first hackle rearward, and in reverse—that is, passing it under the hook and back toward you. The cupped, or dull, side should be facing in the direction that the feather is being wrapped. Tie off the feather and cut off the excess at the position shown.

5. Work the thread forward between the hackle barbs in one step.

6. If done with care, this will upset the hackle little, if at all.

7. Wrap the second hackle in the usual manner—that is, over the hook and away from you. You're winding it right through the first one. Have faith; this will work. If a turn doesn't seat properly, back off and rewrap it.

8. Almost inevitably, you'll have some misbehaved barbs pointing off at bizarre angles. Trim them off, do a whip finish, and you have a Hewitt/Talleur Skater.

ART FLICK'S DUN VARIANT

As to the Variant-style fly, configuring the hackle as was demonstrated on the Skater—that is, wrapping one straightforward and the other in reverse—produces a fly that performs better, and doesn't destroy the leader. Here, Art Flick's Dun Variant serves as an example. Here's the dressing:

Hook:	Regular dry fly, such as the Daiichi model 1180.
Thread:	8/0 Uni-Thread, or comparable.
Tail:	Long, stiff hackle barbs, medium to dark gray.
Body:	Three or four moose mane hairs, one of which is white.
Hackle:	Two large medium to dark gray feathers, opposing one another.

The body is a departure from the original dressing, which specifies a stripped quill from a dark brown rooster cape. I like the contrast obtained from the moose mane. However, it's quite brittle, and an adhesive coating is a must.

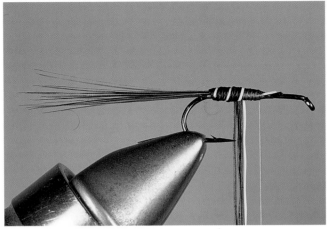

2. Carefully wrap the moose mane hairs, taking care not to let them cross over each other.

3. The oversize hackles are done exactly as was described for the Skater. Don't forget to Zap-A-Gap the body.

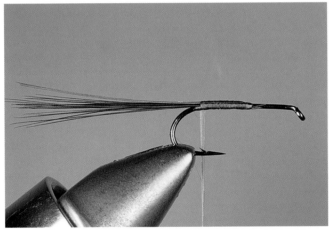

1. Tie on just ahead of the halfway spot on the hook, and make an extralong tail.

Gel Thread and Spinning Deer Hair

16

IN THIS CHAPTER YOU'LL LEARN
1. Working with gel thread.
2. My method for hackling the Bomber.

Working with deer hair has never been my favorite pastime. There's something about handling those bunches of hair and trying to make it do what I want that just doesn't seem like fly tying. But it certainly is fly tying, and those who specialize in it can turn out marvelous creations: frogs that almost go "ribbitt" and baitfish imitations that look as though they could spawn and produce fertile offspring. Reminds me of Geppetto and Pinocchio.

Recently a new, hi-tech thread has come along that makes the job considerably easier and klutz-proof. It's called gel-spun or, simply, gel thread. It's quite a departure from the typical threads we use in general tying. It's

a slippery thread, and hair can be spun over it, almost as though it were bare hook shank. It's also incredibly strong. Don't try to break it with your bare hands, or you may end up in the emergency room.

Two more things to watch out for. First, you'll note that gel thread tends to flatten like minifloss when hanging by the bobbin. That's fine for covering hook shank, but when you want to spin or stack hair, "sharpen" the thread by spinning the bobbin clockwise. On the other hand, if the thread has become narrow due to the twisting caused by being wrapped with a bobbin, and you want to restore it to flatness, spin the bobbin counterclockwise.

As you're about to find out, gel thread must be cut under tension; otherwise, it will slide between the blades of your scissors.

This brookie posed briefly after being fooled by a Kennebago Muddler.

THE KENNEBAGO MUDDLER

Here's a simple Muddler pattern that effectively demos the use of gel thread. It's called the Kennebago Muddler, because of its productiveness on that watershed and others in southwestern Maine. It can be tied in a number of color combinations. Here's one of them:

Hook:	Long nymph or short streamer; here, the Daiichi model 1750.
Thread:	Gel-spun; here, 7/0 Uni-Cord.
Body:	Flat gold tinsel.
Wing:	A mallard or teal flank feather, tied per instructions in the photo sequence.
Head/collar:	Fine deer hair, spun and trimmed.

A note pertaining to hook selection: I like to tie my Muddlers on straight-eyed hooks, because it's easier to trim them at the front without having to work around a turned-down eye. But it's not that big a deal, so suit yourself.

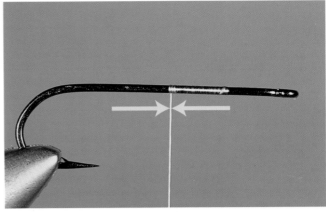

2. When spinning or stacking hair, "sharpen" the thread by spinning the bobbin clockwise, or counterclockwise for lefties. It will resemble that in the photo.

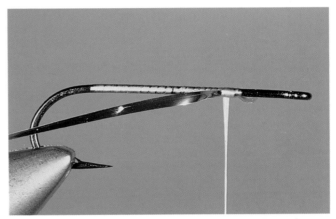

3. Cover the hook with thread, and tie in the tinsel about 25 percent of the hook shank to the rear. This leaves plenty of space up front for the operations to follow.

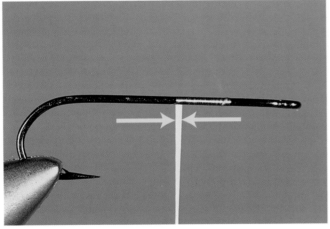

1. Tie on here. As you can see, gel thread naturally wraps very flat. This is great for making neat wraps and creating a very smooth thread base.

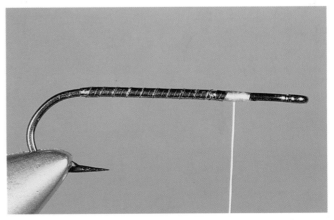

4. Wrap the tinsel to the rear and back, making a smooth double layer, then secure it and trim the excess. Note the little thread base at the front of the body. It's important, as it keeps the feather from sliding forward during the next operation.

5. Strip a mallard flank feather so it resembles the one in the photo, and tie it on over that little thread base with just two or three turns. This is important, as it facilitates the next operation.

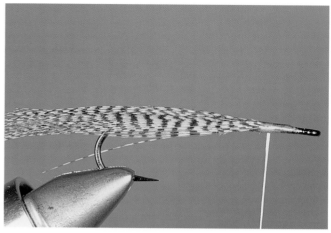

7. With care and a bit of practice, you'll be able to get the feather to fold down slightly around the shoulders of the hook, as shown here. Trim off the excess feather, then wrap the gel thread smoothly to the eye and back to just in front of where the wing is tied off.

6. Take the feather by the quill, and keeping it centered on the hook, pull it forward under the thread wraps. The wraps stay where they are; only the feather moves. Keep the feather centered.

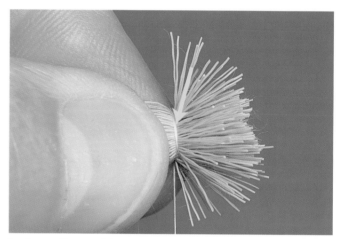

8. Cut off a small bunch of spinnable deer hair, about the thickness of an ordinary pencil. Clean out the underfur and even up the tip ends in a stacker. Hold the deer hair on top of the hook, and take a couple of thread wraps under moderate tension.

9. Take a third wrap and apply tension, flaring the hair. If you want to spin the hair, let go of it. If you want to stack the hair, hold on to it so that it stays on top of the hook. Then take a few more tight wraps to secure the hair, and pass the thread through the butts to the front in one step.

10. Trim the hair to shape, leaving the tip ends for the collar. Apply a droplet of Zap-A-Gap to the finishing thread wraps, and the fly is finished.

THE BOMBER

To further demo the properties of gel thread, let's use as an example the Bomber, which is a very popular type of fly for Atlantic salmon, steelhead, and even large trout.

Hook:	Salmon dry fly; here, the Daiichi model 2131.
Thread:	Gel-spun (7/0 Uni-Cord), finished with regular tying thread; here, flame orange 8/0 Uni-Thread.
Tail and antennae:	Nonspinnable hair, such as goat or calf tail.
Body:	Pulpy, spinnable deer hair.
Hackle:	Dry-fly-quality saddle.

1. Tie on the tail and trim the butts short. Apply a droplet of Zap-A-Gap to the wraps, and rub it dry with a toothpick.

2. Cut off a bunch of hair and shorten it by cutting off the tip ends. This will allow the hair to pass the hook point as it spins without getting snagged. Lay the hair on top of the hook just ahead of the tail butts, and let it shroud down around the hook a little. Sharpen the thread and take two wraps, one atop the other, under moderate tension. With the third wrap, apply firm tension, and let the hair spin. Take several thread wraps

right through the hair on top of the first ones, then pass the thread through the butts and take a few wraps tight to the front of the bunch. If you see that a little underfur was still in with the hair, not to worry; just remove it.

3. Repeat the process, working forward. After spinning on another bunch, use a packing tool or your fingers to compress the hair, so it's as densely packed as can be. A word of caution: Hold on to the spun hair while you pack it, and don't get too muscular. You can push it right off the rear end of the hook.

4. Continue to spin on and compress hair until you have filled the hook shank, but don't crowd the eye, as there's work to do there.

5. Tie off, remove the fly from the vise, and trim the hair into a cigar shape. I recommend curved scissors with serrated blades for this operation. Then put the fly back in the vise, and tie on the 8/0 thread again. Then tie on a small bunch of white hair for the antenna. I find that it's easier to start by holding on to the hair with the right hand and making several lift-over wraps with the left hand. Reverse for lefties.

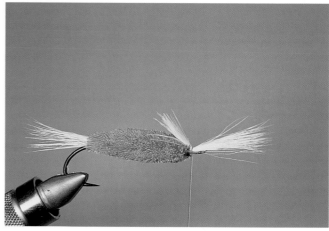

6. Switch hands back to normal, and secure the hair with some tight wraps.

7. Trim the hair butts and cover them with thread. Then take a dry-fly saddle feather and strip the butt end, exposing an amount of quill slightly longer than the body of the fly. Tie it in under the neck of the fly, as shown.

8. Now simply spiral-wrap the hackle, starting at the rear. The wraps bury the quill into the hair. Tie off, trim, whip-finish, and you have a Class A Bomber.

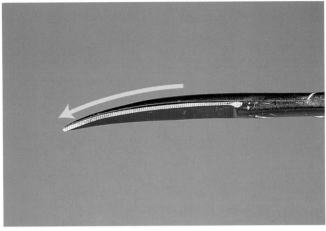

9. My trimming scissors: curved, with a serrated blade.

Gel thread is so potent that you must be very careful when working with really soft hairs. Here's an example. I'm about to spin a bunch of antelope hair. I've taken the encircling wraps, then applied tension. And where did the hair end up? On the table! The thread cut it like a razor. And by the way, that's 12/0 Uni-Cord. Awesome, to say the least.

1. A bunch of antelope hair about to be spun with gel thread.

2. Tension is applied. Hey! What happened to the hair?

3. It got cut in half, that's what!

17

Coq de Leon and Brahma Feathers

IN THIS CHAPTER YOU'LL LEARN

1. Tying with Coq de Leon hen cape feathers.
2. Tying with Brahma hen breast and saddle feathers and Soft Hackle with Chickabou.

One of my very favorite fishing buddies is Mr. Sim Savage of Portland, Maine. While his primary expertise and career experience has been in banking and finance, he is also a licensed Maine guide and ran the L. L. Bean Outdoor Discovery program for a number of years. His beautiful wife, Pat, still works there.

Sim and I have chased trout and salmon to various destinations for quite a while. In the spring of 2003, we spent a week or so at his place on a river that will remain nameless. That bit of discretion, I hope, will enable me to get invited again.

We had hoped for some great dry-fly fishing, but the hatches weren't prolific right then; we were late for Hendricksons and early for whatever was due to hatch next. So, we devoted ourselves to trying out some general patterns of various types. One of them was the Mallard Heron you saw earlier in the book. Tom Whiting had sent me some Brahma hen breast pelts and Coq de Leon hen capes to play with. I incorporated the soft, mottled little hackles of the Brahma into the H-Fly, as we had come to call it, folding and wrapping them as collar hackles to add a bit of contrast.

Sim Savage releasing a Brahma Sutra–caught brown trout.

85

SIM'S SAVAGE SEDUCER

Sim looked over the capes and mentioned that he had a fly he'd used with success for which the Coq de Leon feathers might be just the ticket. He delved into one of his fly boxes and showed me a sample. It was a very simple streamer composed of nothing but grizzly hackle feathers, palmer-wrapped and swept back.

The Coq de Leon feathers did indeed adapt beautifully to this design, and we tied a few on the spot. They worked great! The fly is wonderfully alive in the water, and the trout just couldn't resist eating it. I've named it Sim's Savage Seducer, as he's the one who came up with the pattern. In camp, however, we've given it another name, which will be omitted here. If you'd like to know what it is, approach me in private, and I'll whisper it in your ear. Here's the dressing and the tying instructions:

Hook:	Streamer, 4XL to 6XL; here, the Daiichi model 1750, 4XL.
Thread:	Black 8/0 Uni-Thread, or comparable.
Tail:	Two Coq de Leon hen cape feathers, tied flat against the sides of the hook at the bend, cupped-sides-in.
Main body:	Two to four Coq de Leon hen cape feathers, wrapped palmer style and swept back.

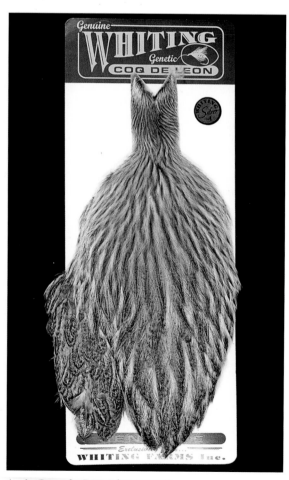

1. A Coq de Leon hen cape.

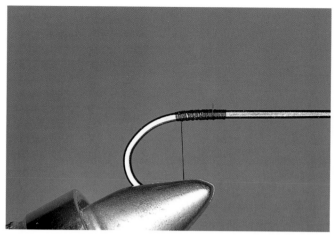

2. Wrap a thread base here.

3. Strip the butts of two feathers from the rear portion of the cape, removing the fluff, and tie them in with the dull, or cupped, sides facing each other, flat against the sides of the hook at the rear.

4. Strip the fluff from a pair of Coq de Leon feathers, stroke the barbs out to 90 degrees from the quill, and tie them in by the tip ends, with the pretty sides facing outward, toward you.

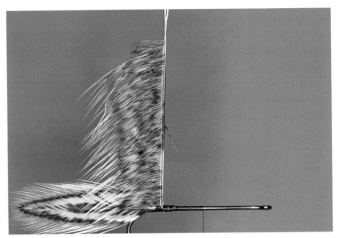

5. Hold the feathers upright with the quill under moderate tension, and fold them by stroking the barbs back. The pretty side of the feathers remains outermost. All barbs should end up on the side of the quill they grow out of; don't let them cross over.

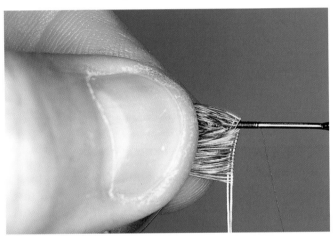

6. Wrap the feathers pretty-side-forward, stroking the barbs rearward as you go, with the quill the leading edge.

7. Add feathers as required to fill the hook, wrapping them as you did the first pair.

8. The completed fly.

Getting the feathers to lie flat against the hook can be a bit tricky. Be sure to wrap a thread base, and if they want to skew while being tied in place, catch a tiny bit of the feather material itself where it joins the quill. If the problem persists, use the trick shown in the Winnie Boy chapter, where a small droplet of Zap-A-Gap is added at the delta where barbs and quill come together.

Sim's fly can be further enhanced by adding a bead or cone. The color may also be varied. Here are two examples: one uses brown-dyed feathers and has a gold beadhead, the other uses olive-dyed feathers and has a black nickel cone head.

One more thought about Coq de Leon. Dr. Tom Whiting has done some very selective breeding of this strain in order to get the feathers to take on certain attributes and markings that fly tiers are looking for. You should be aware that birds from other sources may not have the desired characteristics and may not lend themselves to such applications as this.

A Brown Beadhead Seducer. First, slide the bead into place, then simply follow the previous steps.

You may opt for a cone instead of a beadhead. Here's a little trick that helps fill a cone with thread. Simply hold a needle or pin as shown, and the thread wraps will slide down into the rear of the cone. This locks the cone in place.

A Brown/Olive Cone Head Seducer.

THE BRAHMA SUTRA

About those Brahma breast pelts. Back home, I took a good, long look at them and envisioned how the feathers could be used in a similar manner to the Coq de Leon. The feathers are smaller, but they are beautifully marked and easy to work with. In addition, the pelts had some fluffy feathers at the rear. These are called Chickabou, a registered trade name of Whiting Farms. They are commonly found on various hen pelts besides the Brahma. They are, in effect, mini-marabou feathers and thus very useful, as you are about to see.

I've named this fly the Brahma Sutra. Here's the dressing:

Hook:	Streamer, 2XL to 4XL; here, the Daiichi model 1750, size 8, 4XL.
Thread:	Black 8/0 Uni-Thread, or comparable.
Tail:	One or two Chickabou plumes from the rear of the pelt (Soft Hackle with Chickabou).
Main body:	Three to four Brahma hen breast feathers, wrapped palmer style and swept back.

These feathers are short, so on larger hook sizes, you'll need more of them. I used four feathers to dress the fly in the example. They are webby, so you can space the turns a tiny bit and still get a perfect fill. You can also add a bead or a cone, as was shown on the Seducer. The tying technique is exactly the same.

A Brahma hen Soft Hackle with Chickabou pelt.

1. A Chickabou tail tied in place.

2. A Brahma breast feather ready to be wrapped.

3. The fly is tied exactly the same as the Seducer. Here's the finished product.

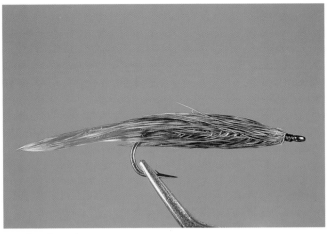

4. The fly when wet.

Dr. Tom also sent me some Brahma saddles. The markings are very similar to those of the breast feathers but are slightly darker and more defined. The feathers run a little smaller, but they are still large enough for tying a small-to medium-size Brahma Sutra. The product name is simply Brahma.

These saddles do not have any Chickabou, but Chickabou patches are sold separately, so you can get the material without having to buy another full pelt. Or you could substitute something else for the tail.

The Soft Hackle with Chickabou pelts are available in dyed colors: olive, golden olive, golden straw, and brown. These dyes are just tints, so they do not obscure the natural barring. More shades may be offered in the future.

Index

Page numbers in italics indicate illustrations.